Keeping Your
Career on Track

Keeping Your Career on Track

Avoiding Derailment, Enriching the Work Experience and Helping Your Organization

DAVID NOER

McFarland & Company, Inc., Publishers
Jefferson, North Carolina

LIBRARY OF CONGRESS CATALOGUING-IN-PUBLICATION DATA

Names: Noer, David M., 1939– author.
Title: Keeping your career on track : avoiding derailment, enriching the work experience and helping your organization / David Noer.
Description: Jefferson, North Carolina : McFarland & Company, Inc., Publishers, 2016. | Includes bibliographical references and index.
Identifiers: LCCN 2016017054 | ISBN 9781476664484 (softcover : acid free paper) ∞
Subjects: LCSH: Career development. | Job satisfaction.
Classification: LCC HF5381.N564 2016 | DDC 650.1—dc23
LC record available at https://lccn.loc.gov/2016017054

ISBN (print) 978-1-4766-6448-4
ISBN (ebook) 978-1-4766-2413-6

BRITISH LIBRARY CATALOGUING DATA ARE AVAILABLE

© 2016 David Noer. All rights reserved

No part of this book may be reproduced or transmitted in any form or by any means, electronic or mechanical, including photocopying or recording, or by any information storage and retrieval system, without permission in writing from the publisher.

Front cover illustration © 2016 Hong Li

Printed in the United States of America

McFarland & Company, Inc., Publishers
  Box 611, Jefferson, North Carolina 28640
    www.mcfarlandpub.com

Table of Contents

Preface	1
Part I: Self-Sabotage	7
1. Derailment by Zipper	8
2. Derailment by Suicidal Meeting Behavior	16
3. Derailment by Political Quicksand	21
Part II: Insight Deficits	31
4. Derailment by Feedback Immunity	32
5. Derailment by Image Mismanagement	41
6. Derailment by Communication Constipation	48
Part III: Faulty Behavioral Wiring	57
7. Derailment by Big Feet	58
8. Derailment by a Big Heart	68
9. Derailment by a Big Head	75
Part IV: Incompatible Needs	83
10. Derailment by the Need to Be Right	84
11. Derailment by the Need to Be Nasty	92
12. Derailment by the Need to Be Busy	100
Part V: Warped Perceptions	109
13. Derailment by Gunnysack	110
14. Derailment by Fantasy	117
15. Derailment by Cross-Cultural Blindness	125

Part VI: Misdirected Loyalties — 135
   16. Derailment by Functional Fixedness — 136
   17. Derailment by Diversity Adversity — 144
   18. Derailment by Sub-Unit Arrogance — 152

Part VII: Dysfunctional Traits — 161
   19. Derailment by Charisma — 162
   20. Derailment by Irrelevance — 171
   21. Derailment by Avoidance — 179

Appendix A: The Derailment Risk Assessment Inventory — 187
Appendix B: The 21 Derailment Risk Categories — 193
Appendix C: The 99 Derailment Hazards — 196
References — 199
Index — 203

Preface

During a post-mortem conversation concerning a high-potential manager who lost her job, it became apparent that I and my friend and colleague Bill Sternberg, senior fellow in leadership education at the Center for Creative Leadership, were, in country western vernacular, well beyond our first rodeo. When we summed the numbers, we were surprised to discover that we had collectively worked with over 30,000 leaders and managers in formal developmental programs and individual coaching relationships.

What didn't surprise us was that over all those years, many of the people we worked with displayed the same career-limiting behaviors (Noer and Sternbergh 2014). These leaders were high potential, bright, and motivated. They represented for-profit, government, non-profit, military, and religious organizational entities. Yet, despite their talent, they were plagued by behaviors that would reduce their promotional opportunities, block their leadership effectiveness, and unless changed, result in their eventual derailment.

I've seen too many talented employees blindsided by the hazards that lead to career derailment. In my somewhat non-traditional career as a human resource practitioner, expatriate manager, CEO, management consultant, non-profit executive, executive coach, and university faculty member I have encountered, and sometimes successfully helped, organizational leaders who found themselves entangled in these hazards. I have even struggled to extricate myself from a couple of them. This book is the result of those experiences. Its purpose is to make those hazards explicit and share strategies to cope with them.

The case studies are based on actual events that I, either individually, or in conjunction with colleagues, have encountered. The names have been changed and occasionally the setting has been slightly altered to ensure anonymity but the examples are valid and the advice offered is grounded in those experiences. I've included additional historical, political, and business examples to illustrate the ubiquity of the 99 derailment hazards.

The derailment hazards represent concrete behavioral examples of the more general traits of arrogance, abrasiveness, aloofness, and untrustworthiness outlined in derailment research (Burke 2006). My approach is more applied. This book distills these abstract traits into real world examples and acts as a frame of reference for specific recommendations and advice for employees at all levels.

The concept of "derailment" as I use it does mean coming off the metaphorical tracks but it doesn't necessarily mean losing a job. It certainly can result in termination, as depicted in many of the examples, but it also can mean demotion, career plateauing, and removal from the fast track and succession planning charts. The deciding factor is elimination of free choice. Derailment occurs by an outside intervention triggered by engagement in one or more of the 99 hazardous practices.

The classic differentiation by Peter Drucker and Warren Bennis, that management is doing things right and leadership is doing the right things (Covey 1989, 101), is unassailable in theory but difficult to differentiate in the shifting contexts and multiple roles that that take place daily in the real world of organizations. In this book, I use the terms interchangeably, although the examples tend to define the appropriate term.

Audience

This book will be of great value to anyone who works in a hierarchical organization. It is not just written for business organizations. I've seen the derailment hazards at work in a variety of organizational settings: non-profit, for-profit, government, military, religious, public, private, large and small. Audiences within these organizations include:

Those in danger of derailing: The 99 derailment hazards lurk in the corridors of all organizational systems. Through public examples and case studies, the book facilitates an understanding of the seductive but toxic power of each hazard and provides specific advice as to how to either avoid or deal with them.

Employees of those who are derailing: For those who work for leaders enmeshed in one of these hazards, the book provides an appreciation of the route their boss has followed on the way to derailment. It offers a frame of reference for evaluating "fight or flight" options: whether to help the boss, wait it out until she derails, or escape before going down with a sinking ship.

Bosses of those who are derailing: For supervisors of those heading down the slippery slope of derailment, it facilitates both an awareness of the dimensions of the 99 hazards, and offers advice that can help save the employee. It provides perspectives that can lead to developing organizational systems and cultures that ameliorate the growth of derailment hazards and provide a healthier work environment.

Helpers of those who are derailing: For helping professionals, external and internal consultants, significant others, and concerned co-workers; the book is a vital resource for appreciating the dynamics of derailment. The case studies and related direct advice will serve as a guide for help and intervention.

Overview of the Contents

I have divided the book into seven parts and three appendices. Each part focuses on an overall derailment dimension and contains three chapters outlining the primary risk categories associated with that dimension. The 99 derailment hazards are discussed in related chapters and do not appear in order of importance.

Part I: Self-Sabotage. This section provides examples of self-inflicted derailment risks and offers perspective and advice on how to stop or repair the damage. The three chapters that cover the derailment hazards caused by self-sabotage are: *Chapter 1: Derailment by Zipper*—career-ending sexual relationships in the work place. *Chapter 2: Derailment by Suicidal Meeting Behavior*—allowing unguarded moments of irresponsible behavior in public meetings to permanently damage careers. *Chapter 3: Derailment by Political Quicksand*—misreading the political climate, over-advocating a previous approach, and lack of flexibility.

Part II: Insight Deficit. This part provides case studies and avoidance strategies for the derailment hazards caused by lack of insight into organizational realities and requisite survival skills. The chapters in this section are: *Chapter 4: Derailment by Feedback Immunity*—the hazards of the inability to "hear," value, or learn from feedback. *Chapter 5: Derailment by*

Image Mismanagement—the career-limiting consequences of a lack of awareness or concern over a projected image. *Chapter 6: Derailment by Communication Constipation*—the derailment potential of not sharing dreams, goals, mental models or development needs and the consequences of a lack of competence in non-verbal communication.

Part III: Faulty Behavioral Wiring. Using the metaphor of the head (thinking), the heart (feeling) and the feet (taking action), the chapters in this section point out the derailment hazards of over-development and reliance on any one of these behavioral preferences. The three faulty behavioral wiring chapters are: *Chapter 7: Derailment by Big Feet*—the hazards of a compulsive bias for taking action, unregulated by thinking or feeling. *Chapter 8: Derailment by a Big Heart*—the career limitations of allowing empathy and emotional support to block rational analysis and decision making. *Chapter 9: Derailment by a Big Head*—the consequences of over-reliance on analysis along with a deficit in taking action and emotional intelligence.

Part IV: Incompatible Needs. This section focuses on leadership needs that, if allowed to flourish, are incompatible with organizational realities and will result in derailment. The incompatible needs chapters are: *Chapter 10: Derailment by the Need to Be Right*—the negative consequences of individual, non-collaborative decision making and stubborn adherence to decisions despite conflicting evidence or other options. *Chapter 11: Derailment by the Need to Be Nasty*—the inevitable derailment consequences of those driven by an ingrained aggressive, intimidating and abrasive leadership style. *Chapter 12: Derailment by the Need to Be Busy*—the career-limiting results of distracting multitasking mania at lower levels and counterproductive "activity traps" toward the top.

Part V: Warped Perceptions. The theme of this part is the hazards of inaccurate perceptions concerning self, others, and organizational realities. The three warped perception chapters are: *Chapter 13: Derailment by Gunnysack*—the devastating personal and career-limiting consequences of accumulating a heavy burden of unvented feelings, emotions, and frustrations. *Chapter 14: Derailment by Fantasy*—the widespread but seldom discussed consequences of judgments and actions warped by false and unrealistic perceptions. *Chapter 15: Derailment by Cross-Cultural Blindness*—the career-limiting hazards of an inability to visualize the different ways country and regional cultures shape employee values and motivation.

Part VI: Misdirected Loyalties. The derailment consequences of inappropriately directed allegiances that don't serve organizationally supportive purposes are the theme of the three chapters in this section: *Chapter 16: Derailment by Functional Fixedness*—the negative result of the application of narrow functional skills and previously successful strategies to new problems that require a different perspectives. *Chapter 17: Derailment by Diversity Adversity*—the derailment consequences of creating narrow, non-diverse work groups and teams. *Chapter 18: Derailment by Sub-Unit Arrogance*—building a team around hostility, superiority, and sarcasm directed at other organizational units or individuals.

Part VII: Dysfunctional Traits. This part focuses on the career-limiting consequences of holding on to leadership traits and values that may have worked in the past, but now block and no longer serve organizational productivity. The three dysfunctional traits chapters are: *Chapter 19: Derailment by Charisma*—inability to modify the "rightness" of a vision or values along with a delusion of invincibility and low tolerance for dissention. *Chapter 20: Derailment by Irrelevance*—skills, styles, and values that no longer fit the current organizational culture. *Chapter 21: Derailment by Avoidance*—unwillingness to authentically engage with employees and escaping into non-essential diversions.

Appendices: The appendices contain a self-assessment instrument that allows readers to measure the potential of career derailment; a summary of the 21 risk categories; and a list of the 99 derailment hazards.

Perspective

Life and career planning is serious business and no one wants to be blindsided. The dangers of career derailment know no organizational or hierarchical boundaries. They are found at all levels, in all types of organizations and I've never met an employee who is completely immune. What separates the best from the rest is a commitment to learning and self-development. If I were to summarize all of the advice in this book into one prescription it would be to understand the reality of the derailment hazards, take the time to look in the mirror, face your developmental challenges, and have the courage to do something about them.

PART I
SELF-SABOTAGE

Pogo the cartoon swamp philosopher had it right when he said, "We have met the enemy and he is us." Employees do it to themselves. Too many fall victim to self-sabotaging behaviors that result in their careers painfully coming off the tracks. The three chapters in this section provide real-world examples and practical strategies for overcoming the hazards of self-sabotage.

Taking your sexual proclivities to the workplace is an extremely risky exercise in bad judgment that is almost guaranteed to unravel your career. A few unguarded minutes in a public meeting or conference can undo years of careful career management and underestimating the political climate and over-advocating a previously successful approach will facilitate derailment.

Part I Chapter Summary

The Three Categories of Self-Sabotaging Derailment Risks and How to Navigate Them

Derailment Risks	What to Do About Them
Chapter 1: Zipper Problems: Sexual relationships in the work place.	No matter how tempting, exciting, or flattering, there is a simple one word mandate: don't!
Chapter 2: Suicidal Meeting Behavior: Allowing brief, unguarded moments of irresponsible behavior in public meetings to permanently damage your career.	Regardless of the seductive aura of informality don't be misled. People are watching and they will remember. Be on your best behavior.
Chapter 3: Political Quicksand: Misreading the political climate, over-advocating a previous approach, and lack of flexibility	Look before you leap. What worked in the past may not fit. Learn to read the signs and let go of strategies that don't fit organizational values.

1. Derailment by Zipper

"Don't get your honey where you get your money."
—*Seasoned middle manager*

Sexual relationships in the work place are always hazardous to jobs and careers. No matter how tempting, exciting, or flattering, there is a simple one word mandate: don't!

"Zipper problems," a generic term for the undoing of fasteners of all types from either gender, have a very high probability of another undoing: that of employee from job. The most common, visible, and, often the most organizationally toxic, are the undoing of zippers between a boss and a direct report.

Hazard 1: Relationships Between Boss and Subordinate

Although one should never say never, in this case I'm going to violate that dictum. I have never seen an affair between a boss and a subordinate end well for either party and, as in the example of the tres amigos, often for the organization.

The Zipper Strikes the Tres Amigos

Brad, Rich, and Wally met in a prestigious east coast graduate school where they were pursuing MBAs. It was the kind of business school where you had to be ambitious, bright, and have a few years of successful business experience in order to get into the school. They set the bar for all three. Brad had worked in urban planning; Rich was a civil engineer; and Wally had financial planning background. All three had roots in Chicago and they quickly bonded to the degree that they were labeled by their fellow students as "the tres amigos," a name they carried back to Chicago along with their degrees.

They formed a partnership and quickly became successful in a business that designed, planned, and managed the construction of public and private buildings, parking ramps, and small airports. As they prospered, they remained tight amigos in both their personal and business lives. They made joint personal investments, all married at about the same time, and formed close relationships with each other's families.

Then the curse of the zipper struck: Rich began an affair with his administrative assistant. She was young, naïve, and seemingly willing. He was middle aged, bored, and should have known better. His partners were shocked, embarrassed for his family, and worried about the stability of the firm and their personal investments. The tres amigos quickly became Rich and two other hombres scheming to find the best way to get him out of the firm. Their spouses were also co-schemers, focusing on ways to help Rich's wife get even for what they perceived had been done to her.

I had a long-term consulting relationship with the firm and considered all three friends as well as clients. They had pretty well sorted out their financial relationships but asked me to facilitate a discussion concerning their future personal and business connections. By the time I became involved a year had passed, Rich's wife was under the guidance of a shrewd lawyer who was looking at him with a greedy expression and a very sharp pencil. Rich's ex-administrative assistant was no longer naïve or willing. Denied a ring, and disappointed with his "whining," she, too, wanted money. The business also suffered. The remaining amigos no longer had the spirit and creativity that stimulated their growth. Rich had formed his own firm and taken some important clients with him.

It was a sad ending. No one was happy, not Rich, not the spurned wife, not the remaining dos amigos, not the rejected administrative assistant and, not me, their consultant. I lost a friend and a long-term client relationship. We were all done in by that zipper.

The lessons are clear. When the zipper strikes, effective teamwork is sabotaged by suspicions, often actual practices, of favoritism and violation of privileged communication. Attempts to keep the relationship secret don't work; the group will always find out and the open secret will erode team cohesion and destroy leadership trust and respect. If either of the participants is married, the team is further sabotaged by operating under an atmosphere of unhealthy collusion.

Hazard 2: Entanglements Between Hierarchical Levels: The Destructive Consequences of Power, Control and Pleasing

When significant differences in power, control, and hierarchical level enter the zipper equation, the second hazard comes into play. Sexual relationships border on, and can easily evolve, into harassment. The three components are power, control, and the desire to please. In most organizations the higher one resides in the pyramid, the more power and control they are perceived to have over those in lower perches. Pleasing the boss is a natural and understandable organizational behavior. When power and control are combined with desire and applied to an employee focused on pleasing the boss and flattered by the attention, bad things happen.

Rita and the Vice President: A Mutually Destructive Attraction

When I was working for a computer firm in Australia, Rita, a young software engineer came to my office in tears. For the past six months she had been engaged in an on-and-off affair with the vice president of product development, her boss's boss and a very senior executive in the firm. He was charismatic and powerful; she was impressed by his power and seduced by his attention. She eventually became disillusioned and wanted to break if off but he wouldn't stop. For Rita, what started as a flattering adventure had become a depressing sentence. Although the vice president hadn't overtly forced or threatened her, the potential was looming. He wouldn't back off, and she was feeling frightened and trapped.

It didn't end well for either of them. After an internal investigation it became apparent that his affair with Rita was but one in a long string of employee dalliances. The firm's managing director tersely summed up the predictable outcome when he said, "We can't keep someone with that problem in a leadership role—get rid of him." He was terminated and Rita accepted an enhanced severance payment as compensation for signing an agreement not to pursue legal action against the firm. Her software engineering expertise was not transferable to any other employer in Melbourne and, since she didn't want to relocate, she accepted a much lower paying position in a different field.

Hazard 3: Lateral Sexual Entanglements

Lateral zipper problems occur between people at the same level in the same organization. If they involve participants that are single, they may seem innocent and harmless, but, as illustrated by the case of Brice and Nancy, they are definitely not.

The Decoupling of "Brancy"

Brice and Nancy worked in the same Los Angeles office, performing similar jobs under the same manager. Their work involved maintaining and troubleshooting computers and training customers on the use and applications of financial information systems. Their somewhat misleading job title was "customer engineer," picked more to impress clients and secure status in the engineer dominated hierarchy of their computer firm, than to describe what they actually did.

They were both single, extraverted, and often traveled together. Long nights, lonely hotels and liberal expense accounts reached an inevitable conclusion and they became, in their firm's jargon, an "item." They became so much of an item that their co-workers merged their names—Brice and Nancy—into a joint entity that they called "Brancy."

With the exception of an episode involving an administrative assistant opening a closed conference room door and discovering what a truly integrated "Brancy" really looked like, for a brief, honeymoon phase, Brancy and the office staff managed to co-exist. As with all workplace zipper relationships, that honeymoon didn't last long. The first episode involved work assignments.

Customer engineers had to live with customers on their sites for a week or more. Before Brice and Nancy's merger, partners were randomly assigned and clients were democratically allocated. Brancy insisted on traveling together and ganged up on their manager for choice locations and clients. In keeping with the manager's conflict avoidance style, she changed her past practices to accommodate them. That didn't sit well with their colleagues. It came to a head during a staff meeting when it was discovered that Brancy not only was assigned a great client, but a trip to Hawaii where the client was opening an Asian support office. Accusations were made, fingers were pointed, and a formerly cohesive team was fractured. A line was drawn and Brancy was alone on one side.

The next episode involved a breach of confidence. Over a beer, a colleague told Brice he was interviewing for a job with a competitive firm and wanted some advice. He emphatically asked him to keep the conversation to himself. Brice's attraction to Nancy overruled his judgment and he told her. She, in turn, told someone else and it wasn't long before it got back to their manager. The word spread that Brancy couldn't be trusted, further eroding team cohesiveness.

It went downhill rapidly. Whenever Brice and Nancy had a spat, which began to occur with regularity, it spilled over into the work group. When the group's manager was transferred to another location, no one from inside the group was considered for her job and many blamed it on Brancy's influence in giving the group a dysfunctional reputation.

I was brought in to conduct a team-building session. After my initial diagnostic interviews with the group members, it was clear that before working on building a team a structural change was necessary: Brancy had to separate. The departing manager finally mustered up the courage to take action. Brice stayed and Nancy accepted a transfer to a lower-level position in a different Southern California location and soon ended up as one of the victims of a large layoff. Then the new manager arrived and her initial priority was to begin the task of rebuilding team spirit and productivity. That meant quickly showing Brice the way to the door. Brice remained in his job for only a month. Brancy didn't survive the transition. Once they stopped working together the relationship ended. Brancy split and Brice and Nancy emerged jobless and depressed. It was a bad ending to two promising careers, all because of that seductive and career-ending zipper.

The simple reality that can be gleaned from the story of Brancy is that there are no good outcomes from workplace liaisons regardless of how innocent they may initially seem. Teamwork is always damaged and boundaries between personal and business issues are blurred. Transfers, promotions, and work assignments are compromised and the inevitable arguments and spats become fodder for work-group gossip and distraction. If one or both parties are married, peer and supervisory perceptions of integrity and trust are damaged and exacerbate an already complicated situation.

Hazard 4: Status-Based Illusion of Immunity

Derailment by zipper has led to the demise of many otherwise talented and creative people. Often it's their very talent and success that promotes a sense of invulnerability. The adage attributed to boxer Robert Fitzsimmons that, "The bigger they are, the harder they fall," holds true. They do get caught and they do fall. One of the biggest, steepest, and most public was that of General David Petraeus.

The Unzipping of General Petraeus

Petraeus, by any dimension of measurement, was a military superstar. A highly decorated four star general, distinguished cadet at West Point, top graduate of the army command and staff college, Ph.D. from Princeton, and commander of the military forces that oversaw operations in Iraq and Afghanistan, he had a meteoric army career. In June of 2011 he was unanimously confirmed as director of the CIA. Just over a year later he resigned, his brilliant career and reputation were done in by that nasty zipper.

Considering his stature and accomplishments, the outing of his affair with his biographer, Paula Broadwell, unfolded in soap opera-like fashion. The components were jealous and perceived threatening emails from Broadwell to a Florida socialite, an email folder containing intimate messages between Petraeus and Broadwell, and an FBI investigation that cumulated with Petraeus being summoned to the White House and President Obama accepting his resignation on November 9, 2012.

Celebrity Zipper Problems: Bad Choices—Steep Prices

Petraeus joins a seemingly inexhaustible list of derailed public figures with highly visible zipper problems who made bad choices and paid steep prices. Tiger Woods lost both sponsors and his credibility as a role model. Bill Clinton damaged his legacy and the integrity of the presidency. John Edwards lost his presidential chance. Anthony Weiner permanently eroded his ethical foundation along with his political future. Bill Cosby lost his credibility as a role-model and eroded his legacy. Although news of political and celebrity derailments dominate the media, top executive zipper problems are equally abundant, and, unlike those in the celebrity world, normally go unreported.

Zipper Derailment Is an Equal Opportunity Hazard

Derailment by zipper is not limited to heterosexual relationships, nor is the male always the initiator or the person in the power position. In a social environment where closets of all varieties are being opened, the hazards of zipper-oriented derailment are exponentially increasing.

A phone call from a former employee I hadn't seen for a few years provides an example. I still remember the brief, but surprising dialogue.

> "What's up—what can I do for you?" I asked after some meandering unfocused conversation.
> "I need a reference," he said. His voice was soft and unusually flat.
> "Why, what happened? I thought you liked your job."
> "It's a long story," he muttered. "It's hard to say." Again, the soft flat voice.
> "Try me," I said. "I've got time."

It turned out that time wasn't the issue; it was the subject. We never quite got to the heart of it on the phone but we did in a face-to-face meeting a week later. After a few beers, "in vino veritas" performed its magic and the truth came out. He was accused of sexually harassing a newly hired male college graduate who reported to him. The new graduate found a savvy lawyer, the firm paid through the nose, and my former employee lost his job. He admitted that the primary reason he hired that young man was because he was physically attracted to him.

When we worked together our company had an unarticulated, but nonetheless clear practice of "don't ask, don't tell." He didn't work for me very long and he was located in a different city so I had no perspective on his sexual orientation. The fact was, I didn't care. As long as he did his job and kept the company out of trouble his private life belonged to him. I, however, declined his request for a positive reference. The reason was not because of his preferences, but because he had allowed that pesky zipper to compromise his integrity.

Derailment by zipper has no biases. Whatever your sexual proclivities, don't exercise them in the office. If you do succumb to the siren song of some form of temptation, the price for your dalliance will most likely be derailment.

Perspective and Advice

- Regardless of age, gender, sexual orientation, or level of management, derailment by zipper is a predictably lethal career-damaging process. You will get caught and it will have dire consequences.
- Remember the wisdom of that seasoned middle manager. Despite the temptation, flattery, or excitement heed his advice: "Don't get

your honey where you get your money," or the more basic version—"Don't get your meat where you get your bread."

- If you are in a power position and are tempted to cross the line with someone lower in the totem pole, know that there are strong odds the person's signals of availability are triggered as much by your role and status than personal attraction. Know also that the odds are even stronger that the relationship will sour and you will pay a heavy price for your dalliance.
- Don't be flattered, misled, seduced by the excitement, or deluded by intentions of someone higher in the organization. The odds are significant that it won't last, it won't help your career, and you will end up as a victim.
- If you continue to be drawn into sexual liaisons within your work place and you can't seem to stop; get help. You have a problem and you need to see a professional.

2. Derailment by Suicidal Meeting Behavior

> "I wish I'd kept my damn big mouth shut and not had so much to drink."—*Morning-after comment by a derailed general manager*

Meetings, celebratory gatherings and conferences, particularly those that are held off-site, involve alcohol, overnight stays, mixed genders and top management, are fertile breeding grounds for a variety of derailment viruses. Too many talented and otherwise self-controlled managers have allowed one brief, unguarded evening to destroy years of careful career development. Given the abundance of corporate war stories concerning employees who have derailed their careers by behaviors such as making inappropriate public passes at colleagues or using alcohol as a lubricant to operate their mouths without engaging their brains, it's amazing that more haven't learned to be on their best behavior at these events. I've seen far too many promising leaders commit unintended career suicide while attending conferences and meetings.

Hazard 5: Unguarded Public Outbursts

As a guest speaker, I had a front row seat to one sad and very public career-ending suicide. It occurred during a large and expensive version of what are known in some corporations as "hundred percent clubs"—celebratory sessions rewarding individuals and organizations that made or exceeded their sales quotas for the previous year. This event took place at a posh resort in Arizona and had expanded to include a large number of support staff. The total number of attendees was over two hundred.

Scoring Zero at the Hundred Percent Club

I knew Hannah from previous engagements at this firm. She was a newly promoted general manager of a small, but important, unit of the corporation.

Prior to the general session she hosted an informal session, including an open bar, with her direct reports. Many of the old hands used the occasion to complain about the corporate strategy along with their perception of the unfairness of the size of the division goals and their own sales quotas. As the first woman to hold a general management position, she felt the need to earn her spurs and be seen by her staff as "one of the boys." She liberally imbibed in the generosity of the open bar and participated in the strategy bashing and complaints concerning inappropriate sales quotas and lack of respect for her division. What she didn't understand was that her division had a long standing subculture of bitching and moaning and no one really took it seriously. Unfortunately, she did, and carried it into the following general session.

The general session was moderated by the CEO and was meant to be the central component of the event. It was a carefully scripted—complete with video clips, music, and snazzy graphics—combination pep talk for the new year and praise and individual recognition for past accomplishments. Regrettably, the new general manager rained on the CEO's parade and ended her tenure on the fast track.

Feeling loquacious from the open bar and amped by the complaints of the old hands, she stood up and interrupted the well-orchestrated performance, pointedly questioning the corporation's strategy, plans for the next year, and ending with a rambling monologue concerning organizational structure and divisional autonomy.

As a speaker at the event and a frequent consultant to the organization, I was asked by the CEO to meet with her and discover "What the hell ailed her?" I posed the question more politely over breakfast the next morning. Amid tears, panic, embarrassment, and lamentation the answer became clear. She drank too much, attempted to impress the wrong constituency—her employees rather than her boss and peers—and, too late, failed to grasp the basic truth that, fairly or not, inappropriate meeting behavior is a prime career derailer. Her accurate, summarizing parting words were that she "wished" she'd "kept her damn big mouth shut and not had so much to drink." Two weeks after the session she was removed from her job and a month later she left the organization, sadder and hopefully wiser.

Hazard 6: Open Public Conflict

A Top Executive Derails by Meeting

Self-initiated meeting-based career derailment is not limited to high-potential junior managers. Jamie Dimon, chairman and CEO of JP Morgan

Chase, and arguably the world's most powerful financial services executive, was fired from a top executive position in the merged Travelers and Citibank organization. His behavior, a public brawl-like shoving match with a rival after an evening of partying and drinking, was the triggering event. One week later he was summoned to a meeting. Expecting role clarification and possibly a promotion, he was blindsided when his former mentor, Sandy Weill, terminated him (Langley 2003). Although he obviously landed on his feet, at that point in his career he was a victim of derailment by meeting. He had previously rejected several outside offers and had no intention of leaving the firm.

Hazard 7: Putting a Bad Entry in the Unwritten Career "Book"

The Unfair Consequences of a Christmas Party

It's not fair, and possibly not legal, but there are many situations where career-limiting behaviors are distorted by oral history and not made clear to the effected employee. Organizations have formal performance appraisals, succession charts, and development plans, but often the "book"—a combination of oral history, hearsay, and rumor—is the deciding factor in determining career progression. This was the case with a plateaued middle-management client who wanted to know why he wasn't going anywhere while many of his peers were moving up.

Written records revealed nothing, but extensive interviewing of past peers and bosses uncovered the reason. Unfair and petty though it may seem, the cause was his behavior at a Christmas party—his politically correct firm called it a "holiday" party—three years earlier. He drank too much, talked too loud, and was rumored to have made a pass at a colleague. Not that these behaviors were appropriate, but the sad fact was that no one talked to him about them and the undocumented "book" on him was that he didn't represent the values of his conservative organization to the extent that future promotions were realistic.

Hazard 8: Underestimating the Impact of "Normal" Meeting Behavior

A Case of Derailment by Staff Meeting Behavior

Career-limiting meeting behavior is not restricted to off-site conferences. As in the case of Barry, it can occur in the context of "normal" meetings. Barry was compensation analyst in a divisional human resources department. He was very ambitious and in the final semester of an evening MBA program. He didn't see himself advancing in HR. He wanted to move out of his staff role into general management. His boss, the HR director, was placed on a three-month temporary assignment to participate in a corporate reengineering task force. During his absence, since Barry was considered a high-potential employee, he was put in charge of the HR department.

The general manager of Barry's division occupied a very powerful and influential role both in his current division and in the corporation as a whole. Barry represented the HR function in this general manager's weekly staff meetings and wanted to use this opportunity to increase his chances of moving out of his HR role. Unfortunately, his meeting behavior had the opposite effect.

He erroneously thought that displaying his newly acquired MBA skills would impress the GM and his staff and differentiate him from just being another HR-type. Whenever a sales or marketing issue came up, he would wax on concerning marketing theory. Whenever a distribution issue came up, he'd pontificate about supply chain management. When the comptroller presented the numbers, he'd interrupt with soliloquies on the value of alternative analytical ratios. The more he talked, the less he impressed the general manager and the further he diminished his promotional chances.

Five weekly staff meetings into Barry's temporary role, the general manager had had enough. He recalled the human resources manager and ordered him to replace Barry and take him off the high potential list. Barry derailed by misreading the staff meeting culture, underestimating the professionalism and knowledge of the general manager's direct reports, and his inability to read the signs. Rather than impressing the general manager and his team, Barry was irritating them.

Although Barry's approach was shallow and immature, his misadventure provides an important lesson. Careers can be made and broken by meeting behavior. It is critically important to assess and never underestimate the power of meeting culture. Meetings are mini-organizations with powerful and usually unarticulated norms and sanctions. Behaving in a way that flaunts and goes against the grain of these norms and sanctions can be a path toward derailment.

Perspective and Advice

- Conferences and meetings are danger zones. Too many carefully planned careers and years of hard work have been erased by one short bout of inappropriate behavior.

- Regardless of perceived casual and permissive norms, careful, conservative, and controlled behavior is essential. Someone is always watching. Don't blow a career by acting as though you are at a sorority or fraternity party.
- Off-site celebratory conferences that combine alcohol, genders, and levels of management, are extremely hazardous. They act as a lens that magnifies other career-limiting behaviors. Abstain or severely curtail alcohol consumption. Never, under any circumstances or peer pressure, consume any other substances. Don't get seduced into knocking the boss, the company, or the strategy.
- Political correctness, abstinence and a positive attitude are the name of the game. They will not only prevent derailment, they will help you stand out from the crowd.
- Meeting derailment may be deferred but it won't go away. Organizations have long memories and inappropriate meeting behavior will be entered into the informal but powerful "book" that more often than not determines your career progression. Don't assume that if nothing is said nothing will happen. If, in retrospect, you regret what you did or said in a meeting, don't ignore it and hope it goes away. It won't; this is one wound that time won't heal. You need to go into damage control mode, make apologies and own up to your inappropriate behavior.
- Don't underestimate the power of day-to-day meetings. It's necessary to develop the ability to read and comply with the unwritten but powerful norms and sanctions of "normal" meetings. Going against them over time can lead to derailment.

3. Derailment by Political Quicksand

"What got you here won't get you there."
—*Marshall Goldsmith*

I've observed too many unsuspecting employees get mired in political quagmires that eventually suck them into joblessness. In today's volatile business environment of mergers, acquisitions, spin-offs, complex strategic options, and activist shareholder interventions, political quicksand can be found at all levels of the corporate totem pole. It lurks in the shadows of boardrooms and executive suites as well as in middle management break rooms.

Hazard 9: Inability to Let Go of What Worked in the Past

A primary survival strategy, as painfully illustrated by Sandra, involves the vision to let go of previously successful practices and values before the weight of them sinks your career in political quicksand.

The Necessary Pain of Letting Go

The inability to let go of a previously inculcated business model or set of values is an increasingly hazardous derailment threat in today's environment of serial acquisitions and mergers. These, from the perspective of many of those in the trenches, "shotgun weddings" may make sense to financial analysts but they inevitably result in conflicts over values and operating processes. Often, they cause the derailment of talented people who are unwilling or unable to adjust to the new reality and perish in post-merger quicksand.

Sandra was the recently appointed head of regulatory affairs for a pharmaceutical corporation. Typical to the industry, her company had grown through a series of acquisitions. Hallway talk referred to this practice as bigger fish continually stalking and swallowing those one size smaller. Sandra's calling card gave a clue to the underlying identity issues: along with the current logo, it contained those of the last two smaller fish that were being painfully digested by her company.

I and a colleague were retained with the plainly stated objective to "help Sandra get with the program." She had spent the bulk of her career with the most recently swallowed fish and that organization's values were firmly, and it turned out, irrevocably, imprinted in her leadership behavior. Her new firm operated from a "numbers trump people" orientation. The only thing that counted was increasing the stock price and the bottom line. Her past employer had an organizational culture that valued the "soft" side. In her new role she quickly learned the names and family history of every member of her large staff. During her initial six months, she invested time, money, and energy in team-building, outdoor adventure training, and interpersonal skill building workshops. In the meantime, the corporate numbers were eroding, and her efforts to secure FDA approval for two new products were taking a back seat to her people-development interests.

When we arrived on the scene, her current marching orders were unambiguous: significantly reduce the number of people on the payroll and personally focus on securing approval for the new products. Unfortunately, Sandra couldn't let go of a past culture that was politically and economically out of sync with her new environment. After implementing a small and insignificant layoff, her staff was still too large and expensive and her personal orientation still remained centered on their welfare and development. Her ending was swift, brutally executed, and abundantly clear. She came to work one Friday, was escorted to the human resources department, turned in her security badge, was given a severance check, was accompanied by a guard to her office where she packed her personal belongings and was on the other side of the front door before noon.

Sandra's derailment highlights a paradoxical good news/bad news situation. The good news is that a strong, cohesive, organizational culture bonds people and promotes a strong sense of identity. The bad news is that a strong, cohesive, organizational culture is very hard to change. In order to avoid derailment by becoming bogged down and immobilized by the quicksand of a culture that is no longer relevant, it's necessary to go through the pain of letting go of values and operational principles that don't fit the new reality. The gain is usually worth the pain. In addition to preventing derailment, learning and personal growth often await those who embrace the new.

Hazard 10: Belief in Top Executive Invulnerability

Yahoo's Executive Soap Opera

Political quicksand thrives at the very top of organizations. The executive soap opera at Yahoo provides a vivid example. In May of 2012, Scott Thompson was fired as Yahoo's CEO after only serving four months. The alleged triggering event was the discovery that he had falsified his resume by claiming to hold a degree in computer science. Strategic disagreement and political infighting with a board member and investor—who was responsible for outing Thompson—was a very strong, if not the primary, contributing factor (Frommer 2012).

Thompson's replacement, Marissa Mayer, lured Henrique De Castro away from Google to help her turn the company around, named him chief operating officer, and summarily fired him a little more than a year later. His severance package, estimated to be more than $60 million, may have set a record for fired executives (CNN moneytech 2014). With a string of CEOs over the past few years and continued concern over financial performance and strategy, Yahoo executives—present and future—need to exercise extreme caution and demonstrate political wisdom lest they too be lured onto the sinking political sands of unplanned termination.

CEOs are supposed to be ethical role models and Thompson's falsification of a resume was a serious violation of this obligation. It's also difficult to feel sorry for De Castro after he walked away with that excessive severance money in his pocket. However, the common denominator is that both were essentially derailed by political quicksand. Thompson was ousted by a boardroom power struggle over strategy and control. If the board member hadn't looked for a reason to get rid of him, his resume doctoring may have gone undetected or less severely punished. De Castro should have been smart enough to never have left Google and joined

Mayer, his former colleague there, if he had doubts about her strategy or their ability to work together. He, too, was derailed by fecklessly treading on the shifting political sands of vacillating leadership and changing strategic initiatives.

Hazard 11: Inability to Read the Structural Tea Leaves

Derailment by political quicksand is by no means the sole province of top executives. A former colleague, Carla, was a very talented human resources manager on a fast-track to replacing the corporate human resource vice president when he retired. She had worked her way up the corporate staff ranks and was a very strong and vocal advocate of centralized control and administration. There, however, was a growing decentralization impetus, fueled by several newly appointed, and described by some employees as, "states' rights, Tea Party–oriented," division managers. They were supported by a newly hired senior vice president. The strategic vision of this evolving group called for decentralizing operations, reducing the size of all corporate functions and distributing their activities among semi-autonomous divisions.

Carla had her feet firmly and stubbornly planted on the wrong structural foundation. It was shrinking and sucking her down with it but she wouldn't back down. The more the political winds blew toward decentralization, the more she moved against them. She was running against the wind and, in her case, the wind won. Had she taken the advice of her colleagues, read the cards correctly, and not fought the inevitable, she would have been named vice president and occupied a smaller but, in terms of power and influence, much more significant executive role than that of the previous vice president. Her constant lobbying and strong public advocacy for centralization shut that door. The new senior vice president succeeded the CEO and replaced the retiring human resource vice president with an external hire. Carla was left hanging in that wind and left the company, derailed by making the wrong choice and sunk by the resulting political quicksand.

Hazard 12: Self-Initiated Political Quicksand—Avoiding Personal Responsibility by Setting Up Conditions for Others to Cause Derailment

Setting Up the Conditions for Becoming an "Out" in an "Up or Out" System: Jake's Self-Initiated Tenure Rejection

The year Jake got his bachelor's degree in business administration the labor market for new college graduates was stagnant and he wasn't sure what he wanted to do so he just kept going to school, eventually earning an MBA with a concentration in corporate finance. Jake was an outstanding student with an evolving interest in research and his academic advisor encouraged him to go even further. He liked and respected his advisor, naturally a finance professor, and was still uncertain about his future, so he applied to several research-oriented universities offering Ph.D. programs in finance. He was accepted at a prestigious east coast university, wrote a brilliant doctoral dissertation, and entered the world of commerce equipped with a newly minted Ph.D. and no work experience.

He got a job with a brokerage firm but soon tired of doing what he considered shallow market analysis and writing, what he considered dumbed-down, overly optimistic reports for potential investors, and quit after a year. The academic world was familiar territory and he accepted a tenure track faculty position with a midwestern university. His new employer was a traditional liberal arts college that had evolved into university status by offering master's degrees in education, health care, and business administration.

The tenure granting procedure in universities is an "up or out" proposition. Beginning assistant professors have a limited amount of time to go through prescribed achievement hoops. While not cast in concrete, the traditional time frame is seven years. Since finance professors are hard to come by, Jake was put on a four-year fast-track tenure program. If faculty members successfully clear the hoops, they are essentially assured of lifetime job security. If they don't they are pushed out the door. Jake's university had three tenure granting criteria: research (measured by publication in refereed academic journals), teaching (measured by peer and student evaluations), and service (measured by serving on university committees and performing administrative tasks).

Research was a snap. Jake published several extremely well-reviewed papers in prominent academic journals. Teaching wasn't a snap, more like a thud. He complained of the "coddled, entitlement-addicted," undergraduate students who thought any grade less than an "A" was an insult and blamed the instructor if they received less. Jake didn't play the "be nice to the students with grades and they'll be nice to you with teaching evaluations" game. He lacked tolerance, political correctness, and was one of the few professors to grade on a strict curve. In return, he received low student evaluations.

When historical liberal arts colleges add professional schools there is always tension. The first cause is salary. Professors in disciplines such as marketing and finance are harder to find and earn larger salaries than their colleagues in fields such as English and history. The second tension inducing stimulus is status. Since there are more liberal arts faculty members and they have been around longer, they tend to have more influence in committees. At Jake's university, many of the old-line liberal arts faculty members looked on the business school as a glorified trade school, without the status and credentials of a "real" academic institution. Finally, there is political tension. The overwhelming majority of liberal arts faculty members are just that—liberal. While often in the minority, what conservatives there are in universities tend to congregate in business schools. In Jake's case, he and just two other colleagues were lonely conservative republicans adrift in a sea of liberal democrats.

If research was a snap and teaching a thud, service was a big, wet, heavy splat, as in a wet blanket being dropped in the middle of his university's curriculum committee conference room. In older, more established business schools, changes in the business core curriculum are vetted and approved by a committee within the business school. As an outdated legacy from an historical liberal arts orientation, Jake's school had a university-wide curriculum committee dominated by liberal arts faculty. As a part of his "service" obligation, Jake was made a member of this committee. He was a dysfunctional and outspoken participant, never losing an opportunity to chastise members for making decisions for which he felt they had no qualifications. When he wanted to make changes in his own finance curriculum, he was frustrated that he had to seek the approval of a bunch of "fuzzy-headed liberals" whose knowledge of finance was stretched when "attempting to balance their checkbooks." He didn't just make these comments in a venting session with his business school colleagues, he shared them with his fellow committee members, thus earning their anger and inspiring their urge to get even.

When I met Jake, two years into his university faculty role, it was clear from his behavior and attitude that he had concluded that the life of a faculty member wasn't for him. He never actually said it; something kept it inside. Rather than just calling it quits, he employed a strategy of self-derailment, sabotaging his career by creating the very political quicksand that would engulf him.

The promotion and tenure committee met the spring semester of his third year and Jake was among six other candidates whose promotion to associate professor, and the concurrent granting of tenure, were on the agenda. Even with all of his political indiscretions and mediocre teaching evaluations, because of his splendid research record and the scarcity of qualified finance faculty, his department chair and the dean of the business school planned on swimming against the tide and arguing in his favor.

Jake must have concluded that there was a possibility that despite his self-sabotaging efforts he might keep his job because two weeks before the committee met, he sent the entire faculty, including all the members of the promotion and tenure committee, an email outlining his perception of flaws in the promotion and tenure system, examples of what he felt were poor decisions made by unqualified liberal arts faculty members, and several radical recommendations that would grant the business school nearly total autonomy. That email was the last, and I imagine, well-planned nail in his academic coffin. Even his dean and department chair couldn't advocate for him after that and he became part of the "out" side of the up or out equation.

Jake ended up working for a large international management consulting firm. It was a good fit but the transition would have been much simpler and less stressful to all involved if he would have taken responsibility for his own career rather than setting up the conditions for others to cause his derailment.

The Bond King De-Crowns Himself

As evidenced by the departure of Bill Gross from Pacific Investment Management Company (Pimco), self-induced career suicide by political quicksand can happen at any level and age. Seventy-year-old Gross co-founded Pimco in 1971 and built it into a gigantic ($1.97 trillion in assets) bond-trading firm. Called the "Bond King" for his investment expertise and outstanding track record, he, from the perspectives of achievement, recognition, and wealth creation, would be considered a spectacular success.

A reasonable career prognosis would have involved grooming a successor, a gradual reduction in work load, and eventual retirement. That didn't happen. Instead, Gross brewed up a batch of political quicksand, leaped into it, and derailed himself. He drove out his heir apparent, Mohamed El-Erian, in January 2014 and embarked on a series of career-ending episodes that would have resulted in his termination had he not resigned on September 26, the day before the trigger would have been pulled.

His self-created quicksand included abusing and yelling at employees, and his career coup de grace was an angry, ten-point email, outlining the company's problems and blaming specific executives. It was sent after the executive committee had warned him to tone down his volatile behavior. Following that email, other executives were described as going one-by-one into the chief executive's office with the ultimatum that either Bill goes or I go. (Grind 2014). They stayed and he went, the victim of his self-created career suicide by political quicksand.

Like Jake, Bill Gross landed on his feet. He Joined Janus Capital Group, a firm only a tenth of Pimco's size in terms of managed assets. He said he was happy to be giving up many of the complexities that go with managing a large and complicated organization. Also like Jake, something kept him from taking the straightforward action of taking personal responsibility for getting what he wanted. Gross didn't need to create the political quicksand that set other people up for derailing him. He could have simply resigned and found a firm that was less "complex" and "complicated" in which to complete the final phase of his career.

The Danger of Approach/Avoidance Career "Suicide by Cop"

The causes of career suicide by creating political quicksand that deflects personal responsibility are similar to those of the well-publicized concept of "suicide by cop": an inability to take personal action, the desire to make a splash, and a need to blame others. While the examples of Jake and Bill Gross are clear, there are many others that are more murky and complicated by an approach/avoidance process. In these situations people set up conditions that would result in derailment, then back away, repair at least some of the damage, and then start all over again. They prepare their own quicksand, step in with only one foot, withdraw and fill it in with gravel, then step around the gravel and step in again with the other foot. The vacillation is confusing to both the participant and the organization. Approach/avoidance quicksand creators require prompt professional help to clarify their motivation and modify their strategy. Unfortunately what often happens is they don't get help and take one step too far into the quicksand, derail and the game ends even though they may have preferred a different outcome.

Perspective and Advice

- Before making a job change, adhere to the adage: "look before you leap." It may look like greener grass over the fence, but it could be a quicksand bog in disguise. Too many normally wise and successful leaders have been seduced into a change only to discover that the same degree of professional due diligence they provided for their employer was sadly lacking when making a personal career decision.
- Misreading the political climate, over-advocating a previous approach, and lack of flexibility can and will lead to a derailed career.
- The most valuable organizational leaders are those who know that what worked in the past may not—and most likely will not—work in the future. In order to avoid derailment it is necessary to remain objective and stay open to the possibility that your past approaches and strategies may not fit the current reality. Accessing others for information and advice is essential but use caution. When that advice leads you to resist change and hold on to the past it will result in the lemming effect: your advisor will join you in the march off cliff's edge.
- If you work with someone who is in the process of self-derailing by creating her own political quicksand, attempt to help her take personal responsibility for career choices, not set up conditions that cause others to act. It may be difficult and require support and assistance, but helping someone own up to their own career options is worth the effort.

PART II
INSIGHT DEFICITS

Whether the cause is a defensive blockage or just an inability to connect the dots, lack of self-awareness is the root of many derailments and is the theme of the three chapters in this section. The inability to "hear" and use feedback to illuminate blind spots is a pervasive hazard to growth and development and a prime cause of derailment. Ignorance of the image one projects and the lack of proactive image management is a derailment factor that too often lurks in the shadows until it is too late to repair. Not understanding the importance of sharing hopes and dreams will result in isolation. Engaging in arrogant and demeaning communication practices will result in alienation. Both isolation and alienation are stepping stones on the path to derailment.

Part II Chapter Summary

The Three Categories of Insight Deficit Risks and How to Navigate Them

Derailment Risks	*What to Do About Them*
Chapter 4: *Feedback Immunity*: Inability to "hear," value, or learn from feedback.	Find and contract with a trusted "truth teller"
Chapter 5: *Image Mismanagement*: Lack of awareness or concern over the image you project.	Assess the image you're projecting against the image you desire. You will need help to make changes.
Chapter 6: *Communication Constipation*: Not sharing dreams, goals, mental models or development needs. Lack of competence and awareness of non-verbal communication.	Take the time and expend the effort to make goals and mental models clear. Learn the power and develop the skills to harness non-verbal communication.

4. Derailment by Feedback Immunity

"I don't need no stinkin' feedback!"
—*Insight challenged workshop participant*

In reference to an old and well-known advertising campaign that told us that a cereal was the "breakfast of champions" and warned us that we'd "Better eat our Wheaties," leadership guru Ken Blanchard (2014) put a feedback twist on that campaign when he stated that feedback is the breakfast of champions. The problem is too many leaders don't eat their metaphorical Wheaties, and without valid assessments of their developmental needs, face the possibility of blindly descending down the slippery slope of derailment. The primary reason that breakfast remains uneaten is that giving and receiving valid behavioral feedback is a dance that requires both parties to hear the same music.

Hazard 13: Unwillingness to "Hear" Feedback

When an Unskilled Coach Gives Feedback to an Unwilling Leader

A memorable example of what happens when both dancers are tone deaf occurred during a group leadership development program. An inexperienced trainer, a recently minted Ph.D., long on theory but short on practical experience, was paired as the primary feedback coach with a chronically disruptive participant who was only in an advanced leadership development program because his boss sent him to get "fixed." It was a bad mix and, in retrospect, I and my colleagues in that program should have known better.

The participant was aggressively defensive, argued, dismissed the value of any feedback, and alienated both the other participants and his feedback coach. The harder he pushed back, the harder the inexperienced coach pushed forward. Things came to a head when, in a moment of uncontrolled frustration, the participant stood and shouted the statement that will live forever in the folklore of those leadership development trainers. Face red and eyes budging, he jumped to his feet and screamed, "I don't need no stinkin' feedback!"

This unforgettable outburst demonstrates two feedback realities. First, those who need it the most often reject it the strongest. This participant really did "need" the feedback and it really was pretty "stinkin.'" He left the session far from "fixed," and his abrasive, insensitive style was nearly certain to eventually derail his career. Second, feedback needs to be given in proportion to the recipient's readiness to hear it and delivered in a manner that reduces defensiveness. The participant was overwhelmed by negative feedback and his coach was unskilled at reading the signs and adjusting his approach.

Hazard 14: Succumbing to Freud's Curse— Feedback-Blocking Defense Mechanisms

Both the feedback coach and the participant who didn't want to touch his "stinkin'" feedback with a ten-foot pole represented extremes. However, even with a skilled feedback coach, many otherwise intelligent, goal-oriented, ambitious leaders, don't solicit or accept feedback that could increase their effectiveness and ward off derailment. One reason for this feedback apathy and avoidance is a blind spot as to its value and an unawareness of the need to take it seriously. Research indicates that some managers on the path to derailment are simply unaware that they are behaving in ways that could lead to derailment (Zenger and Miller 2009). Even when blind spots are removed and feedback is requested, Freud's classic ego defense mechanisms form a powerful deterrent to really "hearing" it.

No one likes to hear behavioral evaluations that are not congruent with their own self-image and defensiveness is the constant enemy of insight and behavioral change. The concept of ego defense mechanisms originated in Freudian theory as processes to distort reality and reduce anxiety but it's not necessary to be a psychoanalytic therapist to understand their impact on feedback.

The Big Three Ego Defense Mechanisms

There are a number of ego defense mechanisms but, in terms of feedback, the big three are projection, denial, and rationalization.

Projection. Projection involves deflecting one's own behavior by seeing it in the actions of others, as in "none of the people in finance are good listeners and they are totally insensitive to the needs of their employees."

Denial. Denial is the refusal to accept the validity of others' perceptions, as in "they're just wrong, I'm exceptionally sensitive to the needs of my employees."

Rationalization. Rationalization is a form of justifying actions by making excuses that no harm has been done, as in "chewing out my assistant in public was good for her; her feelings may be hurt but she'll get over it."

Hazard 15: Lack of the Courage and Wisdom to Look in the Mirror and Absorb What's Reflected

High IQ, Low EQ: A Case Study

The effort to coach Malcolm was unsuccessful but it did serve one purpose: it demonstrated the successful use of the big three feedback-blocking ego defense mechanisms. Malcolm was promoted into a position which could be best described as lower-upper-management. Shortly thereafter, a number of previously unresolved behavioral issues surfaced that, in his new perch in the hierarchy, were much more career limiting than in his past roles.

Interviews with his past employees and bosses, 360 degree assessments, and consultant observation of his meetings and interpersonal interactions unanimously pointed to three potentially derailing behavioral traits. He had a habit of making damaging negative comments about his peers and boss; his new employees felt unusually micromanaged for their level; and some past employees felt he was arrogant and condescending.

Despite much effort and coaching, Malcolm essentially blew off all of the feedback. His new peers were jealous, manipulative, and only focused on their own career progression (projection). His past employees were off-base in their assessment, he was never arrogant or condescending (denial). His new employees needed a kick in the rear and closer supervision. They would be better for it (rationalization).

His company really wanted to save him and they put their money where their mouth was by retaining expensive consultants and paying for external development seminars, but, predictably, Malcolm eventually derailed. The public rationale was that he was a victim of downsizing but the real reason was impenetrable defensiveness that rendered him immune to any developmental feedback.

Malcolm's derailment was a validation of research findings that dysfunctional behaviors that were tolerated at lower levels become more visible, less acceptable, and more likely to lead to derailment at higher levels (McCall and Lombardo 1983). It is also a demonstration of the hazards of allowing defensiveness to block information that can lead to improved performance and career longevity. If Malcolm had only "heard" and accepted the validity of half his feedback, he would still be with the same firm and have a bright future. He was smart and ambitious. If he could have sufficiently lowered his defensive barriers to hear his feedback, he had the intellect to work through his issues and move forward. Unfortunately, his high IQ was paired with a low emotional intelligence (EQ) quotient. Goleman (2006) argues that EQ is equally, if not more, important to leadership success. It takes courage and wisdom to look in the mirror and absorb what is reflected. It takes even more courage along with a high degree of tenacity to learn from what is seen and implement goals to make behavioral changes. Malcolm failed on both counts, the victim of his ego defense mechanisms.

Developmental and Corrective Feedback

There are two types of feedback: developmental and corrective. Ignoring either can lead to derailment. Developmental feedback is information that if properly sent and accurately received can lead to behavioral changes that can stimulate growth, promotional opportunities, managerial productivity, and job security. Good leaders give it continually and savvy followers respond to it proactively. Corrective feedback is much more short term, urgent, and requires a specific response to avoid derailment. In Malcolm's case, as often happens, developmental feedback evolved into the other variety. To paraphrase his boss, shortly before he was fired Malcolm was told, "If you don't stop making negative, destructive public comments about your co-workers, you will lose your job." He didn't and he did.

The Pain and the Promise of Feedback

The pain of feedback is that, even when delivered by a skilled facilitator, it's hard to hear and it always requires the discipline and effort to hold ego defense mechanisms in abeyance. In working with many leaders, I've found that the best way to increase the odds of breaking defensive barriers is to use the three foundational development components outlined by organization development pioneer Chris Argyris (1970): the generation of valid data, free choice about what to do with it, and internal commitment to any planned change. The key to reducing the pain is to allow the recipient to own the data and take responsibility for acting on it. The facilitator is a helper, not a salesman, and the recipient is the owner, not the customer.

The promise is that feedback can and has altered flawed behavior. Most studies are in agreement as to the macro traits that lead to derailment. In a review of the literature, Burke (2006) summarized them as arrogance, aloofness, perfectionism, insensitivity, selfishness and betrayal of trust. Feedback, consistently delivered in a manner that minimizes defensiveness, and received, not as criticism, but as an aid to increasing leadership effectiveness, has the potential to change these career-limiting behaviors.

Hazard 16: Ignoring Corrective Feedback

The Derailment of Douglas MacArthur

President Harry Truman's 1951 firing of General Douglas MacArthur was perhaps the most public and controversial example of derailment for failure to conform to corrective feedback. MacArthur was often publicly critical of his commander in chief's policies regarding the conduct of the Korean War. On December 6, 1950, President Truman, asserting the principle of civilian control over the military, issued a public directive requiring all military officers and diplomatic officials to clear all but very routine statements with the State Department before making them public and to refrain from direct communications on military or foreign policy with newspapers, magazines, and other public media. What happened to Malcolm happened to MacArthur. MacArthur didn't comply and Truman fired him.

Hazard 17: The Trap of the "let me give you some feedback" Approach

Sophomoric Sally: The Wrong Way to Give Feedback

Sally was a bright, articulate, and ambitious human resource manager. Her job required her to wrestle with the myriad dysfunctional and productivity-limiting behaviors that plague most large, bureaucratic organizations. She was intrigued with the potential of the emerging field of organization development to give her tools to help improve things. She was accepted into a highly competitive graduate program that would lead to a master's degree in the field. It was an evening and weekend program, interspersed with several week-long residential sessions. It suited her perfectly because she could keep her job and her employer would pay the tuition.

She was a diligent student, kept up with the readings, actively participated in classroom discussions, and immersed herself in the case studies. Sally was particularly captivated by the second residential session with its primary focus on feedback. She received a great deal of feedback which, because of her desire to learn and the program's training, she received without much defensive blockage. She also practiced giving feedback. She didn't do so well at that. As evidenced by what took place when she returned to work, she needed much more practice and direct, observational feedback on the way she gave feedback.

She returned sophomoric—in the true meaning of that word, she was foolishly wise. She was a feedback-delivering junkie and couldn't wait to apply her addiction to the managers with which she worked. On her first morning back she attended a staff meeting and grew irritated at the negative, self-serving comments of the IT manager. It was a recurring behavioral pattern and she'd had enough. She called him aside after the meeting and angrily confronted him. I was doing some work at her company at the time and observed the interaction. Here is a close paraphrase of that conversation.

"Let me give you some feedback!" she shouted. He shrugged his shoulders, said nothing, and gave her a wry smile. That further fueled her irritation. We were among the now-curious crowd emerging from the meeting and the three of us moved into a vacant office.

"You're always so damn negative. I'm sick of it and you've got to stop," she continued, standing on her toes to make full facial contact.

"I don't know what you mean—why so hostile?" he calmly said, sitting down.

"At the retreat last quarter, you resisted any suggestions to improve customer service. You always say negative things about HR. Everyone thinks you're running your department like a dictator, but because the general manager likes you, no one dares cross you or give you direct feedback. Well, I'm doing it now and it's about time you heard it!"

"Someone's had a bad night, take a valium and get off my back." Again, the voice was calm and the smile lingered.

And so it went for another five minutes. The calmer he was, the angrier she became and the more she dumped stored-up emotional baggage on him. Finally, he told her to go back to her "ivory tower" in HR, stood and left.

"Was that effective?" I asked.

"No," she admitted.

"Who was helped?"

"Me, more than him, I guess. I got a lot of things off my chest."

"Was that really useful to your long-term relationship or to the company?" She just sighed and shook her head.

We went back to her office to review the ground rules of feedback and to come up with a plan to repair the damage. I covered three guidelines for effective feedback along with one general warning.

Feedback needs to be requested, not dumped. "Let me give you some feedback" is a very common and a very bad way to initiate a productive helping relationship. Feedback works best if it is requested, not dumped and is descriptive, not judgmental. That quasi statement is not really a request; it's a prelude to an interaction—usually an angry one that is in the service of the sender, not the receiver.

Feedback must occur close to the triggering behavior. Feedback should be given close to the time of the triggering event. The longer the gap, the less effective the lesson. Sally's feedback was dated and useless.

4. Derailment by Feedback Immunity

Feedback requires specificity and behavioral clarity. Feedback must be specific in terms of who, what, when, and where. It needs to be very clear in describing the actual dysfunctional behavior and the impact it had on others. Sally's situations were too vague and references to "everyone" and "no one," obfuscate issues and serve no purpose.

The three "too"s feedback trap. Sally's interaction was a classic example of the three "too"s prescription for ineffective feedback: her feedback was too late, too vague, and too focused on the sender's, not the receiver's, needs.

Hazard 18: Lack of Courage to Resist Defensiveness and Seek Out the Underlying Message

The IT manager also colluded in an ineffective feedback process. His demeanor and supercilious smile was a defensive mask that blocked his learning. Mature recipients of feedback can help the deliverer send a clear message and know that doing so will be to their ultimate advantage. The wisdom and patience to resist the blockages of defensiveness, the courage to seek out the underlying message, and the skill to help the deliverer be more specific and behaviorally descriptive, are core abilities. Feedback is, indeed, the breakfast of champions and champions have the skills and courage to understand it and do something about it.

Perspective and Advice

- We all have blind spots and wise leaders find ways to illuminate them by accessing the input of others. Regardless of our intentions we all suffer perceptual distortions and it's impossible to accurately see ourselves as others see us. In order to grow and prevent career stagnation and derailment we need ongoing feedback from others.
- It requires patience, tolerance, and self-regulation to truly "hear" feedback. We tend to accept feedback that is congruent with our self-image and reject feedback that isn't and the ego defense mechanisms of denial, rationalization, and projection are constant threats to illuminating our blind spots.

- Wise leaders have the courage, insight, and inner strength to overcome distortions and defensiveness. They continually seek and learn from feedback because they know it is the key to personal growth, organizational effectiveness, and the prevention of derailment. If you are not receiving ongoing developmental feedback from your boss, your peers, and your employees, ask for it and don't settle for letting them tell you what they think you want to hear. It is often necessary to help feedback givers be specific, use behavioral examples, and articulate what you could have done to be more effective. If you argue, deny, or rationalize the feedback, chances are you won't get more and, if you do, it will be so diluted and sanitized that it will be of no value.
- If you are giving feedback make sure the recipient is ready to hear it and present it in clear, non-evaluative behavioral terms, focusing on the situation, the recipient's behavior, and the impact that behavior had on others.
- If you are receiving corrective rather than developmental feedback and want to keep your job, you need to take immediate action. Once you have complied it is essential that you find ways to receive ongoing developmental feedback to prevent being placed in a future "either-or" situation.
- The feedback process is a dance requiring both the giver and receiver to work together and help each other. Without receiving ongoing feedback the threat of derailment increases as a function of both your level in the organization and your time in the job. Without the skills to give non-threatening developmental feedback, leaders won't get optimal performance and will eventually face the harsh reality of making a derailment decision. For the sake of personal growth and organizational productivity, it's essential that both parties learn to dance.

5. Derailment by Image Mismanagement

> "He needs to spiff up his image and start acting like an executive or he'll be history." —*Mandate from a CEO*

The higher leaders reside in the organizational structure, the more people read and often misinterpret their intentions and values. How they dress, what they say, how they say it, what they praise, what they blame, how they use humor, and their body language are all intensely scrutinized and evaluated. Like it or not, image management is an important component of effective leadership and, as was the case with Alex, far too many leaders underestimate its importance.

Hazard 19: Unawareness of an Ineffective Image

Dispensing Executive Bearing: A Success Story

One of my more interesting coaching assignments was responding to the mandate from a board of directors to give Alex, their newly appointed president, some "executive bearing." Executive bearing wasn't something I and my colleagues kept in our office closet that we had the ability to "give" at our discretion. Once we cleared this up with the board and got a better idea of what they meant in behavioral terms by that ambiguous label, we embarked upon a challenging and rewarding engagement. It was challenging because Alex was on the clock; he needed to change or he was out. It was rewarding because he did change and kept his job.

Alex didn't have a college degree but he was bright, entrepreneurial, and good with his hands. He built a moderately successful business designing and building packaging and containment devices for electronic components and computer systems. His business was acquired by his primary customer and he was made president of a newly formed subsidiary, a combination of his old firm and some additional units from his new organization. He reported to a board, chaired by the CEO of the parent company and dominated by other parent company executives. His task was to grow the business both inside and outside of his new corporation.

Executive bearing is one of those abstractions that is difficult to precisely define but one where most people can distinguish those who have it from those who don't. Alex didn't have it and everyone knew it. The acquisition terms assured that Alex would retain the role of president for the first year. Any extension beyond that would be based on mutual agreement. The year was half over and the board was conflicted. They liked Alex's technical skills but were dismayed by the image he presented to his employees and potential customers. The CEO wasn't the most articulate executive we'd worked with but he accurately summed it up when he told us, "Alex is in the big leagues now. He needs to spiff up his image and start acting like an executive or he'll be history." The plot was made thicker because Alex desperately wanted to stay and lead the next phase of the organization he had built.

Our internal code word for Alex was "Pat" because his leadership behavior bore an uncanny resemblance to that of the satirical, deadpan approach of standup comic Pat Paulsen, who began his TV career on the old *Smothers Brothers Comedy Hour*, and actually ran for president of the United States six times beginning in 1968. Like Paulsen, Alex displayed a fundamental disconnect between his verbal and non-verbal behavior. He would stand up in front of his employees and tell them how "excited" he was by the new opportunity while speaking in a slow monotone and looking at the floor. He continued this style with customers and compounded his poor image by neglecting to shake hands or engage in ice-breaking small talk. In group schmoozing sessions, he maintained an inappropriately wide social distance, and shuffled from group to group without engaging with any.

When Alex interacted one-on-one with people he knew and trusted, as he had the leisure to do in his previous role, he was remarkably focused and engaging. It was only when he moved out of his comfort zone—which for him was quite narrow—that he became stilted and lost his self-assurance. Through a variety of techniques such as behavioral rehearsal, role playing, and intensive post-interaction feedback we were able to help him widen that comfort zone. We also arranged for the services of an acting coach

5. Derailment by Image Mismanagement 43

and a fashion consultant to help rid him of his baggy slacks and rumpled sport coats. While all these interventions were helpful, the primary impetus for a changed image was Alex's own determination and resolve. He was simply unaware of the necessity of better managing his image in order to preserve his job. Once he got the message he had the courage to invest the time and energy to change. In a sense, we failed in our initial mandate to "give" Alex some executive bearing. He gave it to himself.

Alex's case was unique. Not that many companies would be willing to expend the necessary resources and not many employees would have Alex's motivation and courage. The case does, however, provide two important lessons applicable to all leaders in all organizational environments. First, image awareness and management is important and without proper attention it can lead to derailment. Second with proper motivation and assistance, images can be managed and achieving an executive bearing that fits the demands of an organizational culture can be achieved.

Hazard 20: Allowing the Need to Be Liked to Eclipse the Need for an Effective Image

Blindsided: A Case Study of Image Neglect

The hazards of image mismanagement are not limited to upper management; they lurk at all levels. Ruth was a lawyer who grew up in Brooklyn and worked for two years in the legal department of a large financial services firm in Manhattan. She was recruited into a supervisory position in the southern headquarters city of a much smaller regional bank. She had a sharp, some would call it sarcastic, sense of humor. As a creature of her culture, she talked fast, moved fast, and used her hands a lot when she spoke. Her New York accent and colloquialisms were sometimes hard for her southern-bred colleagues to decipher.

The technical aspects of her new job were a breeze; her previous experience served her well. Managing and leading her new staff was not a breeze—more like a wreckage-inducing hurricane. She was new in town, single, wanted friends, and made the mistake of hanging out after hours with a group of paralegals who worked for the lawyers who worked for her. Her new employer was very conservative and socially stratified. Managers did not socialize, drink, or gossip with employees two levels down.

Ruth did, and both eroded the trust of the lawyers who worked for her, and confused the paralegals in her new social clique.

She had a strong need to be liked by the lawyers on her staff and rather than earn their respect over time through her leadership and technical competence, she took a short cut and tried to charm them with her wit. They mistook her clever barbs as sarcasm and her informality as a lack of professionalism. The social system both inside and outside her new organization was well-established and networked. One of the longer-tenured, older lawyers who worked for Ruth belonged to the same country club and had long-standing relationships with some of the firm's senior executives. He, accurately, blew the whistle, by reporting that his boss was mistrusted, perceived as flip and shallow, and was going around the legal staff and establishing inappropriate relationships with their paralegals.

The reason Ruth was hired was to bring new systems and productivity-improving processes to an aging, somewhat ossified, legal staff. Despite her short tenure, she implemented several positive changes and senior management was pleased with these efforts but they weren't enough for her keep her job. What they found unacceptable was her image, and image usually trumps accomplishments in conservative, tradition-bound organizations. She was removed from supervision, recast as an internal consultant, and a few months later quit and moved to New Jersey to join a law firm.

The primary lesson from Ruth's venture below the Mason-Dixon Line is the necessity to understand and manage one's image. Ruth was blindsided. She liked her job and, up until she lost it, was unaware both of her image and its power. Had she been aware of the image she was projecting and it's potential to lead to her derailment, with some adjustments to her on-the-job behavior and off-the-job social affiliations, she could have preserved her job and, based on her actual performance, ascended into upper management.

Hazard 21: Viewing Image Management as Selling Out or Inauthentic

Management as a Performing Art

Paying attention and actively managing one's image is not phony or selling out. It is the price one pays for the privilege of leading others.

5. Derailment by Image Mismanagement

Employees expect their leaders to be enthusiastic and positive. They immediately detect any incongruence between verbal and non-verbal communication. They want leaders who walk their talk and are resentful of differences between what is said and what is actually done. They expect their leaders to be clear communicators and active listeners. They want leaders who come across as self-confident but not arrogant. In a prescient book with the intriguing title, *Managing as a Performing Art*, Peter Vaill (1989) pointed out that effective leaders must create and maintain an image that is both a manifestation of their own uniqueness and meets the standards of their audiences: their employees, organizations, and stakeholders

I've found that effective management is indeed a performing art and the form of that art is acting. When working on image improvement, some managers see adapting their appearance and behavior to conform to organizational expectations as inauthentic, phony or manipulative. I help them understand that all jobs require meeting the standards of a job description—whether that description is overt and written or, in the case of almost all leaders, implied and requiring discovery. I have the beginning of the famous monologue spoken by Shakespeare's character Jaques in *As You Like It*, printed on a small card and often ask leaders with reservations concerning the authenticity of performing as a legitimate managerial role, to reflect upon it and relate it to their job. It reads:

> All the world's a stage
> And all the men and women are merely players;
> They have their exits and their entrances,
> And one man in his time plays many parts ...

The part they are playing is leader and if they want to be effective and avoid derailment they need to learn the lines and adopt the required image. That doesn't mean they are selling out or are inauthentic; it simply means they are meeting the required standards of their job.

Hazard 22: Falling Victim to the Impostor Syndrome

Psychologists Pauline Clance and Suzanne Imes (1978) articulated what they called "The impostor phenomenon," which more recently has become popularized as the "impostor syndrome." Originally focused on high-achieving women who doubted their intelligence and discounted their high evaluations, it has been expanded to ethnic minorities and white males. The common thread is that, regardless of positive external validation, those afflicted with the syndrome feel as though they are frauds and don't deserve the success they have achieved.

Joyce Roché (2014, 15) offers an antidote to impostor syndrome that's equally applicable to women, minorities, and organizational leaders who are feeling an imbalance between the role they are expected to play and their self-image. In a cogent one sentence prescription she writes, "Learn to distinguish between the stress of moving up into new levels of responsibility and influence and the conditioned response of impostor fears." The stress is natural; it comes from the outside—the job. The fears and self-doubt come from the inside; they're self-induced and can be conquered by the performing art of acting.

The type of acting that best captures the process necessary to overcome impostor syndrome and relieve the tension between portraying a required leadership image and feelings of inauthenticity is method acting. There are several schools of method acting but what they have in common is integrating the actor's own emotions and past experiences into the character they are playing. In essence they use their past experience to become the player rather than use technique and role playing to pretend they are the character. Impostor syndrome is not overcome by faking it by playing a role where technique substitutes for authenticity.

The lesson equally applies to those attempting to rise above impostor syndrome and organizational leaders attempting to alter their image to one that is acceptable and fits their role. The central task is to not rely on artificial, contrived behaviors, but to holistically integrate their natural personality, emotional orientation, and past experiences into the act of leadership. It will initially feel uncomfortable and may require help from a skilled coach, but for internal harmony and external effectiveness, it is well worth the struggle.

Perspective and Advice

- Derailment by image mismanagement is somewhat of a hidden hazard. It often sneaks up on you. By the time you become aware that you have cultivated an image that goes against the grain of the culture and values of your organization, it may be too late to do

5. Derailment by Image Mismanagement

something about it. The antidote is continual vigilance. The most successful leaders are proactive image managers.

- Many leaders fail to take the time to stand back and assess the image they are projecting. For better or for worse, the image you project can result in success or derailment. Wise leaders don't underestimate the necessity and power of image management.
- Self-delusion is common and can result in experiencing a blindsided reality check. The higher your perch on the organizational totem pole the more filters exist and the more people tell you what you want to hear and not what you need to hear. There is always a gap between your intended image and the perceptions of others. Securing an accurate assessment of that gap is more difficult with each step up the organizational ladder. Successful senior leaders have found ways to continually assess and manage their image on the way up. The less wise face the hazard of an unexpected reality check too late in their career.
- Image management is not a solo act. You'll need help both with the assessment and the change strategy. Feedback is the key to assessment, both formal, as in a structured 360 degree process, and informal, as in asking others. If you are a senior leader it is exceptionally useful to connect with someone who sees you in action and with whom you share sufficient mutual trust to allow that person to tell the truth and for you to hear it. It will require help to process and learn from it, but closely observing the behavior of successful colleagues can be instructive. What is their image? What are they doing to sustain it? How does it differ from yours and how can you emulate it?
- In order to change your image you'll need to change your behavior and it will be extremely hard to do that without the help of a coach. Ideally it should be an internal person who has visibility of your day-to-day behavioral interactions. Some leaders have "contracted" with human resource staff members. Others have enlisted the help of a trusted colleague. Securing the help of a boss or a subordinate as an ongoing coach is a possibility but it is very difficult to sustain a true coaching relationship because of substantial role conflicts.

6. Derailment by Communication Constipation

> "They don't need any of this touchy-feely emotional crap."
> —*Ineffective, irrelevant, HR executive*

As leaders rise in an organization and confront increasingly complex issues, they face the danger of letting their strategic preoccupation get in the way of the necessity of authentic communication. A common problem is that they just don't take the time or feel the need to explain their thoughts, dreams, plans, and goals. All four are important and need to be made very clear to subordinates, peers, and bosses. If you don't take the time and expend the energy to do this, you will be making a solo journey and face the potential of losing the support of those you most need to meet your goals. If you haven't described and worked to co-create the road ahead, others can neither walk it with you, nor help extend it. Without affirmative, authentic communication, you risk the derailment of both your plans and your career.

Hazard 23: Not Sharing Plans and Dreams

Arnie's Unread Mind

I worked with Arnie in his role of president of a newly formed, wholly owned subsidiary of a large technical firm. Arnie's charter was to provide computer-based technical and managerial training, re-engineering expertise, and human resource services to his parent firm. The subsidiary was formed for tax and accounting reasons and his marching orders were to focus primarily on internal customers.

6. Derailment by Communication Constipation

Early in the evolution of this new organization, through personal contacts, Arnie was able to secure orders from two outside customers. This tipped the scales and his latent entrepreneurial orientation surfaced. Arnie wanted to implement a leveraged buyout, spin the subsidiary off, and run his own business. The problem was that he didn't tell anybody. Instead, he spent most of his own time soliciting external orders and ignored maintaining and developing internal relationships. He increased the internal pricing structure to match what some outside customers were willing to pay. This alienated his captive internal customers who were required to use his services, confused his employees, and irritated his boss. Revenues plummeted and expenses increased but, undaunted, Arnie exceeded his staffing budget and hired several new sales people with marching orders to concentrate on the external market.

Within a year, the subsidiary was closed, the sales staff was terminated, and the functions were folded back into the parent corporation. Arnie was relegated into an individual contributor role in an internal staff function— his dream quashed and his management career within that firm derailed. In discussions after his demise, many of his key subordinates admitted that they shared his desire to build an external business but were reluctant to say anything for fear of violating corporate political correctness. His boss and several senior managers, after thinking about it, concluded that spinning off some of those functions could help reduce corporate general and administrative expenses and allow staff costs to benefit from the open market.

Sadder but wiser, Arnie admitted that the reason he didn't share his plans was fear that they would be rejected by upper management and that employees who valued corporate security over entrepreneurial opportunity would feel threatened. His failed strategy was to develop a significant base of external business before coming out of the closet to either his employees or his boss. Had he the foresight to expend the time and energy to share his thoughts, dreams and goals, he would have discovered a great deal of support. As it happened, the price of going solo was derailment.

If he'd shared his plans he would have received some very helpful feedback that would have softened his aggressive tactics and broadened his base of support. Effective leaders need to come to grips with two realities. The first is that people can't read their minds even though they sometimes nod their heads. The second is that they need to create a work environment where subordinates feel comfortable asking for clarification or pushing back on a request. Above all, leaders need to overtly share their visions and mental models and have the courage to alter them if others have better ideas.

Hazard 24: Hiding Developmental Needs

Another form of communication constipation that can lead to derailment is not being open about weaknesses for fear of embarrassment. No one wants to look bad, but keeping people who can help in the dark concerning developmental needs will only make matters worse and, in some cases, can lead to derailment. That's what happened to Richie.

Ritchie's Derailment-Inducing Secret

Richie was a division comptroller who reported to a general manager of a relatively small unit of a textile manufacturing firm. As was the case with most U.S.-based textile firms, Richie's company was facing tough times. Each month the general manager had to present a full-blown report—expenses, revenues, orders, receivables, ratios, and several other key indicators—to the CEO and his staff, including Richie's dotted-line boss, the chief financial officer. The general manager came up through the marketing ranks and financial reporting was not a distinguishing skill so he leaned heavily on Richie to prepare him.

Although Richie had a history of favorable performance reviews, he was not well known to top management. Since there was an addition planned for the CFO's staff and it would have been a significant promotion for Richie, the HR director and the general manager came up with a plan to increase his visibility and expose his considerable financial expertise. They would let him make one of these monthly reports on his own. Richie's morale dropped in direct proportion to the proximity of the presentation. Both his boss and the HR director chalked it up to nervousness and were convinced that, based on his knowledge and comfort with the subject, he would do well.

Richie bombed. He looked at the floor, mumbled inaudibly, lost his place, and based on his meandering, inarticulate responses to questions, left the erroneous impression that he didn't have a basic grasp of the numbers. Mercifully, the general manager rescued him, taking over about half way through and completing the presentation. In a private de-briefing with just his boss and the HR director, Richie owned up to the fact that he was terrified of public speaking and had found ways to avoid it throughout his career. He was embarrassed and didn't tell anyone or seek help. He thought if others knew of his aversion to public speaking it would limit his career.

He was half right. His presentation performance did limit his career. He didn't get the promotion and his chances for another one while that top management team was in office were slim. He was half wrong. Had he not suffered from communication constipation, his boss and the HR director, who both were admirers of his considerable technical and managerial skills, could have helped him develop perhaps not exceptional, but adequate, competence in public speaking. They certainly would never have put him in what turned out to be the break outcome of a make-or-break presentation.

Hazard 25: Lack of Non-Verbal Attending Behavior

Communication is much more than just stringing together words by speaking or writing. Research indicates that over two-thirds of communication is non-verbal, conveyed by body language and voice tone. Inappropriate non-verbal communication can definitely lead to derailment. The risk is compounded because employees are often unaware of their non-verbal messages. Occasionally there are instances when managers are aware, but just don't care. One of my own past bosses, Dr. Smith—his first name was Howard but he didn't let subordinates address him by his first name—provides an example.

What It Meant to Be "Smithed"

When I was promoted to a position reporting to Dr. Smith, I was cautioned not to over-react when I was "Smithed." During my first meeting, I experienced not only what that term meant, but also what being "Smithed" felt like. As I was explaining my plans and communicating how excited and challenged I was in my new role, Smith sorted through a pile of papers on his desk and began reading one. I stopped talking but, while scanning the page, he gestured for me to go on. As I continued, he turned to his computer and began to review his email. I managed to wedge in a few comments between distractions, but he quickly cut me off. He wore reading glasses and, as he stared down at me from over them—his chair was elevated and higher than those across his desk—he thanked me for the visit in a distracted tone, and nodded toward the door. I had just been "Smithed" and it didn't feel good.

I initially thought that Smith's insulting non-verbal behavior was based on his inexperience in the real world of business. He was a transplant from an individually oriented academic research environment and I concluded that he was simply unaware of the impact of his behavior on others. I was partially right; he wasn't entirely aware of his impact. I was partially wrong; his behavior was based not on inexperience, but arrogance. He just didn't care. His agenda was more important than that of others and people were simply objects to be manipulated rather than human resources to be nurtured and developed.

My reporting relationship with Dr. Smith lasted less than two months. My ultimatum to the CEO that it was either Smith or me didn't quite materialize; he kept us both. My function ended up reporting directly to the CEO and Smith became my organizational peer and kept his job. He, however, only managed to hold on for six more months. He treated his other peers in the same manner as his employees and both complained to the CEO. The situation came to a head when the CEO went to Smith's office, for what he described as a counseling session. I accompanied him and observed that he, too, was "Smithed." Smith acted distracted, again leafed through his incoming mail, made no eye contact, and seemed uninterested in the feedback. Dr. Smith soon involuntarily hit the street, a victim of derailment by the non-verbal variety communication constipation.

Dr. Smith was an extreme example but I have observed other careers stalled by the lack of non-verbal attending behaviors. Attending behaviors include body language, eye contact, voice tone, and giving the person you are interacting with the time and space to work through her own agenda before inserting yours. Unlike the experience with Smith, I have found that with help, motivated leaders are able to alter their poor attending behaviors and ward off derailment.

Hazard 26: Inability to Engage in Open, Caring, Other-Centered Dialogue

A Case of Conversational Constipation

Jeff was an artifact of a company culture that found make-work jobs for plateaued, incompetent executives. The HR department was held in low esteem by top management so they decided to park him there for three years until he was eligible for full retirement. As the vice president in charge of such a perceived low-value function, they didn't think he could do any harm. They were wrong on both counts; during the first year of Jeff's tenure, the function was needed to perform a critical task and he did a great deal of harm.

An electrical engineer by training, Jeff joined a start-up computer company right after graduation. He knew one of the more experienced founders and rode his coattails through an unprecedented growth period. He wasn't overly creative or motivated but he knew how to work the "good ole boy" network of early entry engineers and ended up with the meaningless title of "vice president of manufacturing engineering services." He had a nice office, was on several equally meaningless task forces and coordinating committees. He filled his day by attending an astounding variety of non-essential meetings. The retirement of his protector/mentor lead to the elimination of his irrelevant function and his HR holding-pattern assignment.

Jeff had a chronic case of conversational constipation. He didn't have conversations, he made speeches that consisted of rambling "war stories" of past real, or more often fictional, accomplishments punctuated with mind-numbing platitudes. He denied the reality of feelings, approaching all potentially emotional interactions in a fact-seeking monotone strikingly similar to that of the character Friday on the old TV series *Dragnet* where he was seeking "the facts, just the facts."

Two months after Jeff's appointment, his then medium-sized, company was acquired by a smaller, but much more profitable and better managed, firm. Four months into his tenure the organization experienced a downsizing. The company's competitive edge and one of the primary reasons for their acquisition was the core cadre of talented engineers and programmers, all of whom had been exempted from the layoff. There was a strong external labor market and many of these key employees were worried about their future and concerned over the possibility of another round of layoffs. Some had already jumped ship and the new management wanted to stem the flow.

A group of consultants experienced in helping organizations re-recruit layoff survivors was retained. One of their recommendations was a series of small group sessions designed to facilitate the necessary venting and emotional release along with the communication of the optimistic plans for the firm's future. Another recommendation was an individual session be held with each technical professional and either a member of the HR staff or an outside consultant. The purpose of these sessions was to engage in an open conversation, listen to the employees' concerns and demonstrate the company's empathy.

These were relatively straightforward actions that had proven effective with other organizations and, after some facilitator training, would have provided a central empowering role for the HR function. Jeff would have none of it. He didn't want his HR department involved in any "touchy-feely emotional crap." He thought the technical professionals should "stop bitching, and be happy they still had a job." He concluded that the consultant's recommendations were not based on provable facts but on "academic, non-real world fantasy." He wanted them out and since his department had the budget and charter to bring them in, they left.

The results were predictable. Turnover, including some of Jeff's top HR people, skyrocketed. Projects lagged behind schedule for want of technical support. The new management group was not happy. Although the consultants were funded from Jeff's budget, the push to bring them in came from a member of the new management group.

Jeff didn't last a year in his HR role. Because of complications with his employment contract he wasn't fired. He became, of all things, a consultant. In his case that meant he was paid to stay home for two years.

The consultants eventually returned but it was a case of too little, too late. Many of the talented technical professionals left. The company survived and is in a growth mode, but still has not rebounded to pre-layoff levels of either profitability or morale. It's unclear how much of the company's decline can be directly attributed to Jeff, but certainly his aggressive conversational constipation played a part.

Judith Glaser (2014) came up with the intriguing concept of "conversational intelligence." To her, conversationally intelligent people have three traits: they facilitate open transparent dialogue, they are sensitive to others and engage in difficult conversations, and they are open to other perspectives and adapt to new thinking. Jeff struck out on all three and his company paid the price for his low conversational intelligence quotient.

Whether you call it conversational constipation or low conversational intelligence, the outcome is the same. The inability to engage in open, caring, other-centered, creative conversations leads to personal irrelevance, organizational stagnation, and the strong potential for derailment.

Perspective and Advice

- As leaders wrestle with complex change-oriented issues, they face the hazard of letting their action orientation eclipse the need to communicate their thoughts, plans, goals, and dreams to their bosses, employees, and peers. Without the support and understanding of others, leaders are doomed to solo voyages that are prone to derailing both their dreams and their careers.
- If you are a leader, continually remind yourself of the simple truth: people can't read your mind. They may nod their heads, but that doesn't mean they either understand or agree. You need to take the time and go through the effort to make your goals and mental models very clear and have the courage to alter them if someone has better options.
- Hiding an area of weakness will eventually be detrimental to your career. It is far better to find a way to communicate it to someone who can help you overcome it. Suppressing a developmental need until its absence becomes visible and harms your career is a poor strategy that could result in derailment.
- Whether we like it or not, most of our communication is non-verbal and sending the wrong messages can be career limiting. Successful leaders find ways to get feedback regarding the impact of both their conscious and unconscious non-verbal communication. Regardless of your past success, it is very important that you regularly assess and, if necessary, modify your attending behaviors of body language, voice tone, and time spent focusing on the agendas of others.
- The ability to engage in open, other-centered conversations that address difficult issues is indicative of high conversational

intelligence. If you suspect you suffer from this form of conversational constipation, get help. You will need to work very hard to remove the blockages that hinder authentic interactions with others. If you work for someone with low conversational intelligence, they need help. Without it, they and your organization will pay a steep price.

PART III
FAULTY BEHAVIORAL WIRING

Using the metaphor of the head (thinking), the heart (feeling), and the feet (taking action), the chapters in this section point out the derailment hazards of over-development and reliance on any one of these behavioral preferences. Derailment occurs when these body parts are unbalanced. A big head (excessive analysis and thinking) with a small heart (low comfort and limited access to feelings) and tiny feet (unwillingness to take action) will result in derailment. A big heart combined with a small head and little feet will also cause a career to come off the tracks. A big-footed bias for action, unchecked by thinking and feeling, is also a sure recipe for career derailment.

Part III Chapter Summary

The Three Categories of Faulty Behavioral Wiring
Risks and How to Navigate Them

Derailment Risks	What to Do About Them
Chapter 7: Big Feet: A bias for taking action, unregulated by thinking or feeling.	Slow down. Find ways to access others and listen to their thoughts and feelings. Unguided missiles crash. Don't be one.
Chapter 8: A Big Heart: Allowing empathy and emotional support to block rational analysis and decision making.	Management is an against-the-grain experience for the big-hearted. To survive you need to cultivate a support system where you can externalize your feelings and emotions.
Chapter 9: A Big Head: Over-reliance on analysis combined with a deficit in taking action and emotional intelligence.	Difficult though it may be, you need to develop interpersonal competence, empathy, and comfort with the ambiguity and the unpredictably of human behavior. You will need the help of a skilled coach.

7. Derailment by Big Feet

> "He's called 'no toes' because of his ready—fire—aim style. He draws his guns, pulls the triggers before clearing his holsters, and blows off his own toes."
> —*Description of a serially derailed, big-footed manager*

Most managers are rewarded on their way up the organizational ladder by moving quickly, taking individual action and getting things done. Few receive meaningful incentives or positive recognition for slowing down, seeking the advice of others or forming collaborative solutions. An against-the-grain wake-up call that leaders can ill afford to ignore is that the higher they ascend the corporate totem pole, the more individual decision-making hinders their effectiveness and leads to career derailment.

Hazard 27: Taking Action Based on Untested Assumptions

I have worked with executives who have, in retrospect, discovered that they had tripped over their own big feet. Their early conditioning for quick action, unbalanced by deliberation or accessing the advice of others often resulted in leading their organizations more rapidly in the wrong direction. They discovered that less knee-jerk movement into action and more collaboration and reflection would have resulted in taking much more beneficial paths. Some, as in the example of Sarah, have too late recognized that they were playing in a different league where the stakes were higher, the process more complex, and the need to slow down, access others, and tamper down their bias for rapid action was the critical success factor.

Action Before Reflection: Sara's Path to Derailment

Sarah began her career in human resources with a small but growing software firm. She was ambitious and soon discovered that HR was doomed to forever be a dead-end, low-pay, and low-influence position in her company. She found an evening MBA program, signed up, earned her degree, and subsequently was promoted into a management position in financial planning. She was a tough and demanding boss who pushed her subordinates to work harder and faster. Her efforts were rewarded and she was quickly promoted again. This time it was away from her previous staff roles into line management; she was put in charge of a group that revised existing, and developed new, software products. She reported to the chief operating officer who was a few years away from retirement and she had her eyes on his job. The person she most wanted to impress was the CEO who would make the replacement decision. He was quiet and remote and she found him hard to read. His communication style was indirect and the messages were often unclear. One message she thought she heard was his concern with the cost of her new group and their seeming inability to develop any useful new products.

Then came the merger. One morning the senior staff, including Sarah, were informed that the company would be merging with their largest customer. She was smart and knew that, in the world of business, there was no such thing as a merger; it was just a convenient code word to soften up the reality that one firm was taking over another and there would inevitably be staff reductions. She correctly concluded that the customer would be the acquiring organization but that her current CEO would have a strong voice in who was promoted and who kept their jobs. As is the case with most acquisitions posing as mergers, there was an initial period of unstructured ambiguity and that was when Sarah's big feet got her into trouble.

Unable to tolerate the lack of clarity, she defaulted into her action before reflection mode and decided to reduce her staff. Her untested logic was that by getting rid of people she erroneously thought wouldn't be needed by the acquiring firm, she'd be cutting costs and be recognized as proactive and able to make hard decisions. She was wrong. The people she got rid of were those focused on new product development and, contrary to her big-footed bias, they were the very people the new organization wanted to keep.

In addition to reducing their own costs, another reason the acquiring company was interested in Sarah's organization was that they wanted to go into the software business themselves and needed to gain access to people who could help them develop a new generation of products. The acquiring customer organization inexorably exerted control and were clearly not happy with Sarah's decision. She was put in a non-managerial holding pattern and her replacement rehired a small number of the terminated software developers but most of the really talented ones had found other jobs and stayed away. Sarah soon lost her make-work job, allegedly part of the natural process of reducing post-acquisition redundancy, but in reality she was sabotaged by her own big feet. Compulsively taking action based on untested, non-collaboratively formed assumptions can be a fast track to derailment.

Hazard 28: Blindly Following the Signals of a Big-Footed Boss

"Bridgegate": The Perils of Working in a Big-Footed Organizational Culture

Misreading the signals in a big-footed organizational culture can lead to derailment. A highly publicized public example occurred under the regime of New Jersey Governor Chris Christie on September 9, 2013. Christie, noted for his action-oriented, take-no-prisoners approach, was apparently misunderstood by his subordinates, when in unthinking big-footed fashion, they responded in concert to the action before thinking cultural norms and caused massive traffic jams by closing two toll lanes of the George Washington Bridge in political payback to Fort Lee Mayor Mark Sokolich. Bridget Anne Kelly, Christie's deputy chief of staff, Bill Baroni, deputy executive director of the New York & New Jersey Port Authority and a Christie appointee, and David Wildstein, hired by Baroni on Christie's recommendation, all lost their jobs (Little 2014).

Regardless of the validity of allegations of a deeper cover up involving Christie, the "Bridgegate" incident reveals two derailment realities. The first is that there are, indeed, big-footed organizational cultures where taking action that is not anchored in reflection and collaboration is the currency of the realm. The second is that such organizations are hazardous to the career longevity of those who buy into and act out the cultural imperative.

Hazard 29: A Ready-Fire-Aim Style

Serial Big-Footed Derailment: The Saga of No-Toes

No-toes, a Texan who, regardless of the social appropriateness, preferred to wear boots and sport a Stetson, earned his spurs in a rapidly growing firm that supplied components to main frame computers. He talked fast, acted even faster and closed large orders based on unrealistic delivery dates and untested product reliability. When told to slow down, be more deliberative, and coordinate with his company's actual capacity, rather than backing off, he amped up. He ignored the advice and incorrectly accused the director of engineering and the CEO of faulty planning, and was promptly fired.

For all his faults, No-toes was clever. He knew the tricks of both selling computer systems and selling himself to potential employers. During a reference check his former CEO said, "Oh, you're thinking of hiring No-toes." When queried as to the meaning, he explained, "He's an expert at the 'ready-fire-aim' process. He draws his guns, and pulls the triggers before he clears his holsters, thus blowing off his own toes." In spite of accuracy of the label, he was hired by the marketing division of another computer company.

He may not have arrived with all of his toes but he brought his big feet. After an initial spectacular start, he drew the ire of the division general manager by engaging in an unauthorized joint marketing venture with a competitor and was shown the door. He, again, landed on his oversized feet, this time, strangely, as the manager of the branch office of a financial services firm in a large east coast city. In order to accommodate the demands of the public transportation system, the organization had three staggered starting times a half-hour apart. After being there less than a week, he called an all-employee meeting in the cafeteria. He stood on a table and angrily chastised the employees for not coming to work on time. He shouted that he noticed many employees arriving an hour late. He didn't allow time for questions or comments. After the session, he put his big, digitally challenged feet on the floor and, fishing for a compliment, asked a subordinate, "How did I do?" When told he'd just made a public fool of himself, he blew it off and canceled the flexible start time policy.

It was only a matter of time before No-toes found himself on the street again. I was involved when he re-applied and was wisely turned down by the computer company. The saga of No-toes illustrates that a big-footed, "ready-fire-aim" strategy may work well in some environments for a limited time, but will, over time, only result in sore feet and derailment.

Hazard 30: Fabricating a Problem to Justify Taking Action

The Lesson of Iraq

Some leaders are so driven by their need for taking action that they either fabricate or deceive themselves into truly believing in a non-existing causal problem. Justifying the March 20, 2003, invasion of Iraq on the existence of weapons of mass destruction is the most public example. There were no weapons of mass destruction. In retrospect, then Secretary of State Powell described some of the intelligence as deliberately misleading (NBC 2004) and Former President Bush said his biggest presidential regret was the intelligence failure in Iraq (Goldenberg 2008). History will judge whether there was an actual intelligence failure, or if self-deception based on a latent big-footed need to take action, was the real stimulus.

Hazard 31: Shallow Diagnosis— Self-Serving Analysis

False and deluded assumptions that trigger big-footed actions are by no means restricted to complex geopolitical issues. The business world is filled with hard-wired, big-footed managers who, regardless of their validity or relevance, are very creative at finding causes that fuel their compulsion to move into action.

"Short-sticking" and a Big-Footed Manager: The Tale of James and Ollie

I ran into James a number of years ago when I was working for a large international oil company. He was the midwest manager of retail sales and his primary role was to increase the sale of gasoline and other petroleum products through what the company preferred to call "service stations," but what most employees labeled "gas stations." He was responsible for

7. Derailment by Big Feet

several hundred stations and had five area managers reporting to him. One was Ollie, who was once his peer, but now was a subordinate.

At the time, it was exceptionally hard to find dealers to lease the gas stations that were owned by the company. Lessees needed to make a substantial personal investment, be willing to work very long hours, and, even though the company touted them as "independent businessmen," they were contractually required to do the company's bidding and buy only their products. James's greatest fear was closed stations. If the door was shut, gas didn't flow and his quota performance dropped. Then, there was the toll on his reputation and career progression. Corporate executives didn't like closed stations; in addition to the lost revenue, they were unsightly and diminished the company's image.

James often found himself in an adversarial relationship with the credit department. The credit manager worked out of his midwestern office, but, unlike everyone else in that location, didn't work for James, but reported to a corporate credit function in New York. The kind of dealers James's area managers were able to recruit usually weren't the most creditworthy and many could not come up with the capital to pay for their first shipment of gasoline. The only way to get them started and keep them in business was to give them their gasoline on consignment. That meant that the company would put gasoline in the dealer's storage tanks and the dealer would only pay for what was sold, taking a small per-gallon profit. This required granting the dealer a large line of credit, a privilege not bestowed on many in their previous lives.

Ollie wasn't necessarily demoted; he just remained in place while others moved up. He and James were both area managers and good friends. When James was promoted, Ollie ended up working for him. Congruent with his big-footed orientation, James made some immediate changes, one of which was moving Ollie to a different area management position. It was one with more stations which James thought would increase Ollie's visibility to top management and enhance his promotional chances. Ollie did get the visibility, but it was the wrong kind. In less than a year, Ollie's area led the region in closed stations and suffered a significant drop in sales volume.

The midwest credit manager had a difficult balancing act which he performed with dexterity. He had to help the sales force keep the gas flowing by granting consignment credit lines while maintaining reasonable conformity to the guidelines issued by his New York boss. Until James took office, his relationship with the past midwest sales manager was a workable check and balance affair, lubricated by mutual trust and openness.

James's big-footed analysis of Ollie's problem consisted of one short meeting where he did much more sending than receiving. What he sent was his understanding that the decline in business and the excessive number of closed stations was the result of the credit manager's long standing grudge against Ollie. Ollie didn't need to work very hard to fuel that fire. He just misrepresented an event that had taken place two years previously, which, in reality, was the result of Ollie's fudging numbers on a credit application.

James then used this shallow, inaccurate analysis as a stepping stone to an even less thought through big-footed plan to enhance his own career and solve, what he believed to be, a structural issue with the credit manager's reporting relationship. James wasn't well known to the senior executives in New York, but what they did know they liked—his sales figures were positive and he seemed aggressive and decisive. So, when he asked for a meeting with the senior credit executive and the three top managers in the sales function, they agreed and set it up.

In what he thought was a show of decisiveness, innovation, and tough-minded management, James blamed the decline in sales and the excessive station closings on the midwestern credit manager's refusal to grant consignment credit to Ollie's area because of a personal grudge. He recommended that the credit manager be fired and that his replacement report to him. James had come up through the ranks of the closed, insular midwest retail operation where his big-footed, hip-shooting style was tolerated and often worked. This was his first interaction in the company's big leagues and it was neither tolerated, nor did it work.

The check and balance credit reporting system was a corporate standard and top management was not about to change it. The midwestern credit manager was a model employee and was on an accelerated development plan for promotion to New York in the next year and James's grudge accusation lacked credibility. What the New York executives decided was to perform an operational audit. That meant sending a small team to Ollie's area to check out the facts before making any decisions—a distinctly non-big-footed approach.

What they found was that James had a huge blind spot when it came to Ollie. His big-footed analysis and problem definition were not only wrong, but reflected a lack of the due diligence expected of managers at his level.

The problems were not credit related but due to Ollie's sloppy and undisciplined management. The smaller size and less visible nature of his past assignment had masked his basic incompetence.

The only credit-related issue they discovered was his dishonest "short-sticking" policy. Because of their lack of credit worthiness, many of Ollie's dealers were on a semi-weekly collection schedule. This meant that Ollie or a representative had to physically place a measuring stick in the dealer's storage tank. They would measure the number of gallons sold and collect the money due the company. The short-sticking occurred when they under-reported the number of gallons sold and collected less than what was owed. It was a type of consignment Ponzi scheme, where Ollie would mask the fact that the dealer didn't have the funds to pay for the gas he had sold along with the shared delusion that somehow he would come up with the money to make up the difference.

Short-sticking was a "fireable" offense and Ollie lost his job. Irresponsible big-footedness did not appear on the company's list of behaviors that led to termination, but three of its components—false accusation, inadequate analysis, and shallow diagnosis—were more than enough to derail James's career.

Like James, hard-wired, big-footed managers not only use the "ready–fire–aim" sequence to orchestrate their actions, they use it to develop a rationale for that action. Their compulsion to act causes them to bypass rational analysis and find causes that support their need to do something. Whether doing that something is supported by fact, fiction, or delusion is beside the point.

Perspective and Advice

- The organizationally conditioned compulsion to move rapidly into action, unchecked by reflection and collaborative discussion, is a somewhat good news/very bad news proposition. The good news is that it is often rewarded at lower, less complex and strategically important organizational levels. The bad news is that it is a predictable route to derailment at higher levels.
- Far too many ambitious, big-footed mid-level leaders move into action based on unchecked assumptions of what their boss or the

organization really desires. If you want to impress those higher in the pyramid, it is essential that you slow down and perform an extensive, multidimensional (your boss, your peers, and your employees) assessment of what is really needed and what will be rewarded. Moving too quickly into action without understanding the consequences is, more often than not, a career derailer. Difficult though it may be for those conditioned to big-footed action, doing nothing while seeking clarity on true needs and contingent rewards, is far better than doing something. Seductive though moving quickly into action is, it is often the siren song of derailment.

- Beware of big-footed organizational cultures. They can be found in start-ups where a risk-addicted founder enjoys betting the company and rolling the dice. Self-contained units of larger organizational systems when lead by an action-oriented, non-reflective boss are breeding grounds for a big-footed sub-culture. They can survive only as long as the primary organization serves as a financial and strategic buffer. Political organizations with assured funding—either through outside sponsors or taxpayer money—can evolve into big-footed cultures. The necessary additional ingredient is a leader who has a need to be seen as decisive, action-oriented, and punitive to those who oppose her.
- If you find yourself working in a big-footed organizational culture, don't be seduced by the excitement. The thrill is not worth the potential derailment and damage to your reputation. Your best strategy is to get out before the inevitable implosion.
- If you manage a talented, but no-toed employee, the good news is that you may be surprised by some spectacular successes. The bad news is that unguided missiles will eventually land and are prone to cause unplanned disasters. The pain of keeping an unreformed, no-toed employee on your team is not worth the gain. You either need to buck the odds and help him keep his lower digits in tact or bite one of his bullets and get rid of him.
- If you look down and discover missing toes, chances are your career has had some highs but far too many lows. If you are honest with yourself, you'll discover that the lows have been caused by your ready–fire–aim habit. To put it simply, if you desire a sustainable career, you need to stop operating your feet before engaging your head. Channel your compulsion for action toward yourself.

Don't be afraid to seek professional help. You will have a difficult time keeping those guns holstered on your own.
- If you work for someone who is so driven by his need to take action that you suspect he is either fabricating a causal problem or deceiving himself into really believing it exists, you have a fight or a flight option. Fighting means you need to help rid him of both his compulsion and delusion. In my experience with most big-footed managers who manufacture causes, while not mission impossible, helping is very, very difficult and requires time, money, and professional assistance. Flight is a more realistic option. It requires either finding a way out of his organization or distancing yourself and waiting until he inevitably derails.

8. Derailment by a Big Heart

"No good deed goes unpunished."
—*Oscar Wilde*

Hazard 32: Inability to Make Hard "People" Decisions

Too Nice a Guy: The Dynamics of a Big-Hearted Derailment

Floyd was endowed with an oversized heart that eventually lead to his derailment. I had the unpleasant duty of facilitating a meeting between him and his boss, a vice president of retail banking operations. She denied him a salary increase and put him on probation for, in her words, "being too nice a guy."

"Probation," in the bank's lexicon, was shorthand for providing the necessary documentation for demotion or termination. Since there was nothing in the bank's performance appraisal system that indicated being excessively nice was grounds for such harsh actions, she needed to be much clearer concerning her criteria for these decisions. Floyd was African American and both the human resource and legal functions were worried about a potential discrimination suit.

The legal action was a needless worry since one of the issues that held Floyd back was his pattern of tenacious avoidance of any form of conflict. It was difficult to entice him to meet with his boss at all and, without the help of a third-party facilitator, he would have deflected any form of confrontation. He was, what organizational psychologists Waldroop and Butler (2000) call a peacekeeper: someone who is determined to avoid conflict at any cost.

8. Derailment by a Big Heart

Despite Floyd's issues with power and conflict, his employees loved him. He was an excellent listener, wonderful at reflection, paraphrasing, and attending behaviors. He was always positive, polite, and courteous. Active in several community service and charitable groups, he could always be counted on to adjust work schedules when his employees needed time for similar activities. Unlike most managers in the bank, he didn't work his way up the ranks; he'd been selected for his supervisory role from a pool of new college graduates. He'd been a community activist and a social worker prior to returning to school and completing his degree in sociology. His position at the bank was his first in the business world.

He cleverly managed to side-step the normal day-to-day conflicts that face all supervisors. Those that didn't solve themselves, he delegated upward and this was the first red flag for his boss. The performance appraisals he submitted for his direct reports were all glowingly positive with no semblance of a bell-shaped curve—another red flag. There was an incident when a relatively large client demanded lower fees and threatened to go to a competitor if he didn't get them. Changing the fee structure would have a ripple effect with other customers and a difficult decision was needed. Every time the employee in charge of the account went to Floyd with the issue, she'd be overwhelmed with empathy, sincere reflective re-statements of the problem, and affirmations as to her own competence, but receive no resolution. The first time the employee felt good, but left with no decision. The second time she felt frustrated, and again left with no decision. The third time, she left angry and beat a path to the vice president's door.

The decisive blow was the layoff. The economy took a dive and the bank's net profit followed. Their reliance on marginal real estate loans came back to haunt them. The decision came down from on high that each department was to reduce their workforce by a minimum of ten percent. The cuts were to be distributed across organizational levels, salary grades and functions—no exceptions, no deviations. It was not the best way to implement a layoff but the die was cast, and everyone was required to comply.

Floyd resisted. He articulated a long string of reasons; his people were too important; it would hurt families; harm the community. Like the residents of fictional Lake Woebegone, everyone in his department was above average. Whenever an employee would meet with him to express concerns Floyd earnestly listened and reassured that person that he would not be laid off. Unfortunately, this assurance was given to most of the people in his department. The cut list was eventually made by the vice president, not Floyd, and the message was passed on to those who had to go by a member of the HR staff. Floyd couldn't do it.

The vice president had more than enough examples to document what "being too nice a guy" meant in operational terms. Floyd was demoted and transferred to a non-supervisory job in public relations. A few months later he resigned to accept a job with a much better "nice guy" fit: director of a non-profit community service agency.

The saga of Floyd provides a classic example of the dynamics leading up to derailment by an oversized heart. Big-hearted leaders are "nice" people. They care about others, have excellent interpersonal skills, and are able to form empathetic relationships. They are the kind of people with whom you'd feel comfortable sharing a personal problem, letting them take care of your kids while you took a vacation, or just meeting for a casual after work drink. When it came to leading your organization through turbulence and making hard business decisions, you'd be much less positive. If one was your boss, you'd like him as a person but grow weary of his inability to forge a decisive path through conflicting polarities and eventually develop immunity to his flattering personal affirmations. In their profile of CEO derailments, Dotlich and Cairo (2003) describe this behavioral pattern as "the nice guy syndrome," and use Motorola's ex CEO, Chris Galvin, as an example.

Hazard 33: Avoiding Necessary Conflict

Jimmy Carter: The Spectacular After Life of a Big-Hearted President

A public example of the fate of a big-hearted leader was the presidency of Jimmy Carter. He has been described as a "better man than a president" (Pile and Roberts 2014, 366). He masked his inexperience by paying too much attention to details and, in classical big-hearted fashion, avoided conflict and was seen as indecisive. Once freed from the against-the-grain burden of the presidency, his big heart allowed him to soar. In 2002 he received the Nobel Peace Prize for his work to solve international conflicts, advance human rights, and promote social and economic development. Three other presidents have received the prize, but, interestingly, President Carter was the only one to receive it for his activities after he left office.

Hazard 34: Over-Reliance on Feelings and Emotions

The Achilles Heel of Big-Hearted Leaders

The primary cause of derailment for the big-hearted is their discomfort with decision making that discounts feelings and emotions. Managing is an against-the-grain activity for those with oversized hearts. It requires the type of objective decision making based on thinking and not of feeling. A widely used assessment instrument, the Myers-Briggs Type Indicator (1998), measures, along with other personality dimensions, whether decisions are made based on thinking or feeling. Among the general public, the split is roughly 50–50 with women having a slight preference for feeling. Among mangers the overwhelming decision-making preference is thinking among both male and female managers. In a study of more than 22,000 managers (Carr and others 2011) reported a whopping 86 percent based their decisions on thinking.

Harvard psychologist David McClelland (1987) developed a well-known theory of motivation dealing with the relationship of the needs for achievement, affiliation, and power. His research indicated that successful business leaders had a moderate need for achievement, a low need for affiliation, and a high need for power. This profile does not bode well for either happiness or career longevity for big-hearted business leaders since they thrive on affiliation and are uncomfortable with power. This pessimistic prognosis for big-hearted leaders is supported by research on based on the FIRO-B (Schnell and Hammer 1993), an assessment instrument that measures wanted and expressed needs for affection, affiliation, and control. Normative data from a sample of over 3,000 participants (Hammer 2000) indicates that the need to control others was by far the highest of the three expressed needs for managers and increased by managerial level.

Hazard 35: Against-the-Grain Seduction by Status and Money

"A Lover, Not a Fighter; a Healer, Not a Wounder": The Fall and Partial Rise of Ben

When Ben graduated, through his participation in his university's ROTC program, he was commissioned as a second lieutenant and entered the army. Although he liked the discipline he didn't fit the stereotypical image of a soldier. He majored in psychology and became friends with his advisor, an industrial and organizational psychologist who, when he found that Ben was going in the army, hit the nail on the head when he said that Ben was a "lover, not a fighter," and a "healer, not a wounder."

The army is a large organization with room for many roles and Ben found a niche that fitted his advisor's characterization. He helped develop and actively facilitated a program that emphasized the "soft" leadership skills of listening, coaching, empathizing, and self-awareness. Ben always argued that the so called "soft" skills were really "hard," a perception not usually shared by the hard-bitten mid-career officers who were sent to his classes to smooth down their hard edges.

When he left the army, Ben was hired by a non-profit research and training organization and given the task of building on his military experience and developing a leadership development program that would have commercial appeal, add revenue to the organization and value to the program participants. He was exceptionally successful and his course offerings became the primary source of funding for the institution. Concurrently, Ben became more and more a manager and less and less a designer and a facilitator.

His advisor's description was, indeed, prophetic. Ben "loved" designing and facilitating and hated the strife and "fighting" that accompanies any managerial role. Turf battles, conflicts between his direct reports, with his peers, budget issues, and the need to enforce performance standards took a toll on his big heart. Complicating matters, he'd married a woman with a much smaller heart and bigger, more ambitious feet. She liked his status—he'd been made a vice president of the organization—and his salary. Although the non-profit couldn't provide stock options, he was paid quite well when compared to other non-profits.

Seduced by his success and pushed by his wife, Ben moonlighted by starting his own consulting business and offered leadership training programs weekends, during vacations, and through adjunct staff. The harder he worked, the less he liked himself. In reverse of what happened to the fabled Grinch, Ben's heart grew ten sizes smaller. He was tired, chronically irritated, and drinking too much. Things came to a head when his non-profit organization hired a new president who immediately ordered Ben to stop offering competitive courses on his own time.

He went downhill fast. He quit his job, lost interest in both his consulting business and his wife, and descended deeply into the bottle for solace. He stayed on the bottom for a few years but, happily, through his involvement with Alcoholics Anonymous and encouragement from a new wife, has surfaced and is doing big-hearted work as a counselor at a rehabilitation center. There are three lessons that can be gleaned from the saga of Ben:

Big hearts are easily wounded. Authenticity and openness invite vulnerability. If you are among the big-hearted, you need to find a big-hearted support system and avoid the seduction of roles that diminish your gift.

Managerial roles in all types of organizations are hazardous to big hearts. Working in a non-profit organization will not provide immunization to the vulnerability of big-hearted managers. All managerial roles require making hard decisions and relying more on analysis and logic than feelings and emotions.

Money, status and power are the seductive siren songs of derailment. Big-hearted employees need to rigorously guard against diminishing their self esteem and wasting their gifts by abandoning their values. Financial and status rewards are possible, but are not worth the price if they require sacrificing big-hearted ideals.

Perspective and Advice

- The reality is that nice people often do finish last in the business world. Despite many theorists' infatuation with participative, emotional, and "soft" management, thinking, using power, and exerting control are the currency of the realm in business leadership. If you are a big-hearted leader, you're a duck out of water in the business world.
- There are some very effective big-hearted business leaders but they are a relatively scarce commodity and they pay a heavy psychological price for continually behaving against their true grain. If you're one of them, the key to organizational survival is the cultivation and maintenance of an effective support system. "Sucking it up" and not externalizing your natural frustration is a very bad strategy. You need to find an outlet; someone or some group you trust that possess the skills to facilitate your necessary venting. Without the ongoing help of a viable support system your bottled up emotions

will cause serious psychological problems and your job performance will decline.
- Using a key subordinate to make and communicate hard decisions is not a useful long-term strategy. It may work for a short time but it's difficult to sustain over the long haul. The leader still has to live with the consequences of hard decisions no matter who makes or communicates them and the resulting role confusion makes a complicated process even more confusing. If you are a big-hearted leader you need to step up to the plate, endure the consequences, and seek venting and relief through an external support system.
- Non-profits, particularly those that are small and community focused, can offer the best of both worlds for someone who is hard wired to be big-hearted and wants to lead. They, too, require difficult people-oriented decisions, but they tend to be more collegial and supportive of big-hearted values.
- If you work for a big-hearted manager don't expect him to run interference for you when the going gets tough and brutal people decisions need to be made. You will get an abundance of empathy and personal affirmations, but little support when you're between a rock and a hard place and need help. If it appears that your big-hearted boss is there for the long term, strongly consider a transfer. You won't learn anything about the real managerial world and you face the prospect of being labeled as a pushover based on your identity as a member of what has sometimes been labeled a "wimpy" organization.

9. Derailment by a Big Head

> SPOCK: I prefer the concrete, the graspable, the provable.
> KIRK: You'd make a splendid computer, Mr. Spock.
> SPOCK: That is very kind of you, Captain!—*Star Trek*

The Spock-like world of big-headed leaders is one of logic, data, and rational analysis. Feelings and emotions are extraterrestrial irrelevancies. Since big heads nearly always come equipped with small ears, they have been described as "emotionally tone deaf" (Waldroop and Butler 2000, 149). The *Star Trek* series derived much of its dramatic effect from the interplay between the data-oriented, big-headed, emotionally void Vulcan, Spock, and the big-hearted Doctor McCoy. What's needed in today's turbulent organizations is a hybrid of both Spock and McCoy. Without sufficient emotional intelligence, big-headed leaders face significant derailment potential and without a grounding of logic, and data-based analysis, big-hearted leaders are ineffective.

Hazard 36: Over-Reliance on Data: Under-Reliance on Feelings

Why Spock-Like Leaders Derail

Big-headed, Spock-like leaders derail for two reasons, the first is that, whether they like it or not, leadership involves dealing with people, not things, and people have feelings, emotions, and human needs for affirmation and empathetic connection. The second derailment hazard is the trite but true "analysis paralysis." Leaders seduced by endless measurement, benchmarking, and analytical processes fall on their statistical swords when decisions need to be made and action taken. Big-headed leaders far prefer meshing the statistical gears inside their oversized craniums to taking action. The example of Nelson's derailment illustrates both factors: his lack of empathy, and his inability to escape from the safe seduction of measurement and move into more risky action.

Hazard 37: Addiction to Analysis

Nelson's Big-Headed Derailment

A caricature of Nelson would show a very big head, a small heart, and tiny feet. Educationally, he had a Ph.D. in electrical engineering from a midwestern school grounded in prairie empiricism: the paradigm that, if it couldn't be measured, it didn't exist. He came up through the technical ranks in an aerospace firm. He was a brilliant design engineer and had successfully secured patents and developed several new proprietary products. He had reached to top of his technical pay grade and, in order to give him more money and reward his past accomplishments, he was promoted to a management role. He headed up the firm's newly established consulting division. The mission of this new venture was to sell engineering and software consulting services to other firms.

The employees of this division were not a volunteer army; they were drafted as part of a corporate strategy to reduce general and administrative expenses by selling services to outside organizations. My role, along with some colleagues, was to help this new division make the difficult transition from an internal cost center to a profitable external consulting firm. The adjustment was compounded because, in order to stay afloat, they needed to sell their services back to the parent corporation and many of them had no desire to be external consultants in the first place.

The issues the management team of the new consulting division brought to Nelson's attention during their first scheduled monthly meeting were that many of the employees were unhappy with their consulting roles, internal clients were balking at their billing rates, and that there were few external sales. Nelson asked them to do a pricing analysis of competitive firms and told them to explain to their internal customers that they had always paid those rates but that they were now "unbundled," with visible "burden" costs.

9. Derailment by a Big Head

By the third meeting, things had become substantially worse. Internal customers were building their own staffs and retaining outside consultants. Several of Nelson's most talented employees had accepted other jobs. The pricing analysis yielded no significant information and the internal customers didn't care about accounting "burden rates." Not explicitly stated, but clear to an observer, the management team members were depressed and frustrated. Rather than acknowledge their feelings, Nelson told them to do a process flow analysis of their internal procedures and measure the sales productivity of the consultants. He paid no attention to their gloomy body language and made no attempt to thank them or acknowledge their hard work under very stressful conditions.

By the eleventh meeting, the division was facing a severe cash flow issue, losses had risen exponentially, several more consultants and one manager had quit, internal business had dried up, and the remaining managers were clearly burned out. Based on Nelson's direction, the division had completed a process flow analysis, halfheartedly implemented a total quality management process, established a laborious sales call monitoring system, benchmarked other consulting firms, and were in the process of developing a confusing and complex performance management system.

There was no twelfth meeting. Nelson's boss, the company's chief operating officer, concluded that a year with Nelson at the helm was enough. His replacement successfully executed a just-in-time damage control strategy and turned the division around. He downsized the staff, concentrated on a limited number of competitive products, eliminated revenue dependence on internal business, and established supportive, participative relationships with those managers who remained.

Nelson took a severance package and eventually joined a startup firm in a pure technical capacity. When I last met with him, he still hadn't gotten the message through his large thick cranium. He articulated a big-headed version of "if only." "If only" we had done the right market and product analysis; "if only" we'd done a more in depth analysis; "if only" we had the time to implement a better total quality management system; "if only" those managers weren't "so sensitive."

Why Big-Headed Leaders Are an Endangered Species

Not all big-headed leaders are as clearly dysfunctional as Nelson. In the past, many managed to survive and, at times, thrive. Two things have changed and the consequences have made big-headed leaders an endangered species. The first is the impact of re-engineering and the subsequent epidemic of downsizing. Many organizations are populated by angry, demoralized, and risk-averse layoff survivors (Noer 2009). The skills it takes to re-recruit and help these wounded survivors move back into productivity and help them focus on customer needs instead of their own survivor symptoms are not the traditional planning, directing, and organizing skills of the past.

The second change is the nature of the workforce. Highly skilled technical workers have many employment options. Unlike the old psychological employment contract, they don't sign up for life and don't expect to stay with one company throughout their career. Emotionally void and overly analytical leadership will drive them out. In order to avoid derailment and be relevant to the needs of today's employees, leaders need to move beyond the analytical and quantitative skills they learned in MBA programs and become proficient in helping skills.

Big-headed leaders face the challenge of going against the grain of past cultural practices that actually reinforced the very behaviors that, today, can lead to derailment. They need to overcome four substantial historical barriers. These are presented as derailment hazards 38–41.

Hazard 38: Inability to Drop an Affinity for Macho, Analytical, Controlling Cultures

In many past organizations, "real" (non-staff, line) managers did not reflect feelings or deal in empathetic dialogue. They analyzed and controlled. Empathy, collaboration, and "touchy feely" relationships, may have been valuable, but they were the tools of "staff types" and not found on the tickets that needed to be punched on the way to the top.

Hazard 39: Left-Brain Bias

The right side of the brain controls our emotional and intuitive perceptions and behaviors. The left brain is involved in analytical, rational thought and it clearly bulges out on big-headed leaders. In the United

States and most other Western cultures, organizations have a strong left-brain bias that results in an overemphasis on formal logic, analysis, and rationality. In most organizations, even with the increasing evidence of the utility of emotional intelligence, IQ trumps EQ and helping skills are much less valued than controlling and analyzing skills.

Hazard 40: Perception of Management as a Science

This is not scientific management as defined by Frederick Taylor (people can be taught to work systematically and can be factored into the production equation similar to machines). Rather, it has to do with the inferiority complex felt by business schools and management training institutions in relation to scientists and their subsequent overreaction as they, too, tried to be "scientific." There was, and unfortunately still is, in many institutions the idea that you can study humans the same way you study rocks. Anything that was intuitive, feeling, or smacked of our unique human spirit was driven out of business education for fear that it would look weak and not seem "scientific." Unfortunately, this focus has produced graduates with the very skills that, unless balanced with a helping orientation, can lead to eventual derailment.

Hazard 41: Fear of Softness

At the zenith of the old paradigm there was a reaction to anything that was deemed "soft." This included feelings, relationships, empathy, and anything that was "touchy feely." What was valued were facts, figures, and statistical analysis—"hard" stuff. Even though such rock-ribbed disciplines as physics now report that facts are relative, the bias continues. Organizations still talk about human resource and training as the "soft" side of management. But, not only are people issues as real as financial and production figures, they require just as much skill and strength. They also require authenticity and the risk of self-disclosure. This is much "harder" than hiding behind a memo, a stack of figures, or a quantitative decision matrix.

Hazard 42: Narrow Scope—Compulsion to Measure and Control a Single Paradigmatic Box and an Inability to Think Outside of It

Robert McNamara—Trapped Inside the Box: The Derailment of the Biggest Big Head

Former Secretary of Defense Robert McNamara was the most public and, in terms of impact, the biggest of the big heads. Serving under Presidents Kennedy and Johnson, his analytical, quantitative, systems-oriented approach facilitated the escalation of the Vietnam War and he was often called its architect. Along with McNamara, Vietnam derailed President Johnson, and exposed a basic flaw in the big-headed leadership paradigm.

McNamara, a Harvard MBA, accounting professor, and veteran of the Air Force's Office of Statistical Control, became president of Ford Motor Company in 1960. He and his close associates adopted the moniker "whiz kids" for their big-headed, statistically-based, analytical management style. It was an approach he carried over to his role of defense secretary. The basic flaw of the whiz kid approach is its insular, internal nature. Big-headed leaders are seduced and blinded by their compulsion to measure and control only the contents of their paradigmatic box. The inability to look outside the box leads to their ultimate demise. In his telling memoir McNamara clearly describes the trap of making decisions within a box of supposed values without stepping back and assessing the validity of those values:

> We of the Kennedy and Johnson administrations who participated in the decisions on Vietnam acted according to what we thought were the principles and traditions of this nation. We made our decisions in light of those values. Yet we were wrong, terribly wrong [McNamara 1996, xx].

Perspective and Advice

- Spock-like leaders who are emotionally tone deaf derail for two often interconnected reasons. Either they are unable to form empathetic relationships and relate to the human needs of their employees or they succumb to endless analytical loops inside their large heads and are unable to escape into the real world of decision making. They are frequently the victims of faulty selection criteria,

chosen because of their technical skills or as a reward for past individual achievements.
- In many organizations, past obsolete cultural norms reinforced leadership practices that, in the new reality, lead to derailment. Big-headed leaders that came up under the old paradigm and wish to avoid the danger of derailment in the new, face the challenge of behaving counter to the style that got them where they are. They often require external help to step out of their paradigmatic box and see the career-limiting consequences of big-headed leadership.
- If you are a big-headed leader and wish to remain in your role, the first step is to make a conceptual leap. The essence of leadership is dealing with people not sterile abstract data. People are messy: they have feelings, emotions, and human spirit—all that touchy feely stuff. In order to lead them you need to play on their turf with interpersonal competence, empathy, and comfort with the ambiguity and unpredictably of human behavior. For most, it's a long, against-the-grain, uphill slope. It's an easier climb if you have the support of a coach.
- If you work for a big-headed boss you need to guard against being seduced by analysis paralysis. Despite your bosses proclivity, you will need to make decisions and take actions without all the data she requires because there will never be enough. If you need emotional support, compliments, and pep talks, look elsewhere; you won't get them from her. If you have an oversized heart and you sense your boss isn't going away, you should. A big heart working long term for a big head is at best a recipe for constant frustration. At worse it can lead to serious emotional issues. The pain is not worth the potential gain. Get out.

Part IV

Incompatible Needs

Whether acquired through misguided early career conditioning or external psychological factors, some leaders find themselves crippled by personal needs that are incompatible with organizational success. The need to be right, germinated by insecurity and fueled by arrogance, blocks personal growth and limits careers. The need to be nasty is toxic to individual and organizational productivity and will lead to derailment. The need to be busy is a career-limiting distraction to middle managers and can be damaging to entire organizations at upper levels.

Part IV Chapter Summary

The Three Categories of Incompatible Needs Risks and How to Navigate Them

Derailment Risks	What to Do About Them
Chapter 10: The Need to Be Right: Individual, non-collaborative decision making and stubborn adherence to decisions despite conflicting evidence or other opinions.	Have the courage to drop the veneer of invulnerability and personal "rightness" and open yourself up to others.
Chapter 11: The Need to Be Nasty: Driven by an ingrained aggressive, intimidating and abrasive leadership style	Muster up the courage to look in the mirror and don't back away from what you see. It will be difficult and you'll need help but unless you make some fundamental changes it will only be a matter of time before you're gone.
Chapter 12: The Need to Be Busy: Distracting multitasking mania at lower levels and counterproductive "activity traps" toward the top.	Drop the façade of busyness. Organizations want people who can focus, appear calm, and have time to authentically connect with other people. Beware of becoming caught in an activity trap. Seek external help to escape.

10. Derailment by the Need to Be Right

"There are not enough Indians in the world to defeat the Seventh Cavalry." —George Armstrong Custer

Bright, ambitious people whose self esteem is based on their need to be right are predestined for derailment. Their brightness and ambition, when combined with a lack of interest in understanding and learning from others, traps them in a delusion of omniscience. The derailment of Maria provides an example.

Hazard 43: Linking Self esteem to Unilateral Rightness

Done in by Her Need to Be Right: Maria's Rapid Rise and Fall

Maria was bright—a master's degree in math and Ph.D. in computer science—both from prestigious ivy league schools. She was ambitious, driven, and enjoyed a dramatic ascent in the business world, rising from programmer analyst to vice president in a multinational computer firm in ten years. At the age of forty, she convinced a venture capitalist firm to take a chance and started her own software firm. For the first year her remarkably successful career trajectory continued. Her firm grew in both revenue and employees. Then she came off the tracks. Her derailment was as rapid as her ascension. She was done in by her need to be right.

She had a binary, either/or personality. For her, things were black or white. There was no grey in her world. She was a first-generation Hispanic American and from elementary school on, her values were formed by one

10. Derailment by the Need to Be Right

basic motivational mantra; you were either successful or a failure, either on top or on the bottom, either right or wrong—no in between.

Her quantitative education reinforced her orientation. For her, there was no subtlety, ambiguity, or contextual differentiation. Things either were or they weren't. Vacillation, accessing others, and deviating from her own sense of rightness when making decisions were not only a sign of weakness; they were a refutation of her earned credentials and an admission of failure. And, if there was one thing that threatened Maria's self esteem, it was failure. In her either/or identity, she was either right or a failure. There was no middle ground.

Her ambition, intellect, and ability to make rapid individual decisions played well in the scientific, quantitative engineering culture of her company and paved the way for her swift ascent into upper management. It also impressed the venture capitalists and led to their funding and taking an equity position when she started her own business.

A little after a year into her new enterprise, the venture capitalists began to hear rumors of discontent among the senior technical staff. This concerned them because they had acquired additional equity in Maria's business and, although revenue was growing, expenses were growing faster, and profits were not meeting expectations. The top techies were very marketable and were key to delivering on past commitments and securing new business. The bankrolling capitalists did not want them unhappy or leaving the firm to join competitors. They didn't get their wish. A very talented software designer left Maria's company and joined her primary competitor. After talking to the defecting designer, the managing partner of the venture capital firm asked for assistance diagnosing and overcoming any problems.

Morale was bad throughout the firm and increased by organizational level. It was at its worse among Maria's direct reports. In her previous role as an employee of a large, over-structured organization, she was rewarded on the way up for prompt individual, non-collaborative decision making. She got things done and that was the promotional ticket. Once she reached upper management the bureaucratic structure buffered and acted as a counterbalance to her unilateral, arbitrary style. Now that she was on top of her own organization there were no structural constraints. Her latent approach was unleashed and the organization paid the price.

Her staff was afraid and told her what she wanted to hear which was always congruent with her own self-formed opinion. She had no tolerance for ambiguity which effectively suppressed any open dialogue around complex and context-laden strategic alternatives. Giving her feedback on these issues was like talking to a plant, and making progress on behavioral change was akin to walking east down the aisle of a 747 flying west. I wasn't making any progress and was about ready to tell the venture capitalists to stop wasting their money when the critical incident that blew her off the tracks occurred.

A much larger Asian conglomerate with business interests well beyond Maria's core software business had been making acquisition overtures. On the surface the deal appeared very attractive. It would result in a fresh infusion of capital and open a number of new product distribution channels. There were also some strong negatives. Control would move out of the U.S. and alienate some current customers. Jobs would be lost to lower-cost Asian workers and there was much concern about the buyer's true intentions; many suspected they would simply exploit the existing technology and customer base and close U.S. operations entirely.

The venture capitalists didn't want to do the deal. Her staff didn't want to do the deal. An outside accounting firm, retained to assess the value of the company, recommended against the deal. Maria, trapped as she was inside her ego protective bubble of "rightness," did the deal anyway—or, at least she tried.

Without informing anyone, she signed a preliminary agreement, called a press conference, flew in a top Asian executive, and announced the acquisition. The problem was that she didn't have the authority. She was president and technically reported to a board chairman who didn't normally become involved in any management decisions. He, however, had invested in the firm and, together with the venture capitalists, controlled a slight majority of the shares. Since, in the past, he had rubber stamped all of her decisions, she took him for granted. This was an assumption where her rightness compass pointed the wrong direction. He sided with the capitalists and killed the deal.

There were two results. The first involved heavy legal and public relations fees along with a face-saving, expensive but essentially meaningless, contractual relationship with the Asian suitor. The second was Maria's departure: a prime example of derailment by the need to be right.

As Maria's rapid ascension and sudden demise illustrates, the need to be right is both seductive and toxic. For bright ambitious people it can be a fast track to the top. However, once there, the environment is too complex and ambiguous to rely on any one person's conceptualization of rightness.

10. Derailment by the Need to Be Right

Collaboration, accessing others, and understanding the limits of one's own judgment and cognitive capacity are essential components of individual and organizational survival.

Maria's wild ride also demonstrates the power of early conditioning and ego defense mechanisms. She based her identity on standing out, being right, and rising above her humble first generation family circumstances. That motivation is difficult to alter and Maria never did. She is now a tenured professor at a research-focused university where her rightness goes unchallenged by her students and her colleagues.

Hazard 44: Letting Ego and Arrogance Block Valid Data and Other Opinions

The Spectacular Derailments at Waterloo and Little Bighorn

Derailment by the need to be right is not the exclusive domain of the world of business and commerce. History is filled with examples. Two of the most spectacular are those of Napoleon and Custer.

Napoleon's defeat on June 18, 1815, at Waterloo not only changed the course of European history, it spawned a word that has become synonymous with spectacular derailment. Meeting your "Waterloo" has come to mean, not just derailing, but going down in flames.

Ignoring staff warnings concerning the Prussian army's resurgence, Napoleon asserted his own judgmental rightness, scoffed at his enemy's capability and presided over what has been described as a silent breakfast. It was silent because he was confident of his own rightness and brokered no further discussion. He postponed the attack until the afternoon, giving the enemy time to reach the battlefield and appointed what some historians perceive as second rate commanders to conduct the battle. His conviction of his own rightness along with his unwillingness to access others, directly contributed to his defeat and spectacular derailment (Libert 1995).

On another late June day, 61 years later, George Armstrong Custer's belief in his own rightness combined with a need to prove himself, resulted in the annihilation of five of the Seventh Cavalry's companies with a total casualty count of 368 dead and 55 wounded. Keeping his own counsel, he rejected the offer of assistance from the Second Cavalry, refused to bring in a battery of Gatling guns, and ignored the assessment of his own Crow scouts. His ego and his arrogance were seen by many as the roots of his demise (Philbrick 2010).

Blocked Classroom Learning: A Waste of Time, Money and Opportunity

Custer and Napoleon didn't attend a formal classroom-based leadership development program, but if they had, they may have followed the path of a recent participant, who like too many others, used his belief in the rightness of his own self-perception to block necessary learning.

Unchecked, the need to be right can mutate into a delusion of omniscience, devaluation of alternative perspectives and blocked learning opportunities. The aforementioned participant told the group he didn't want or need any feedback on his leadership capability and was only in the program because his boss made him come. He didn't engage with his peers and clearly communicated the message that he was "right" in knowing what he needed to do be successful and it certainly wasn't learning about himself or accessing others. Perhaps he was a distant relative of Custer or Napoleon.

He lost a lot. He will not be part of that group's future network, losing access to helpful colleagues and potential customers. By ignoring the feedback of his peers and their rich conversation concerning organizational issues, he lost the opportunity to learn about himself and broaden his perspective on organizational behavior. The money his company spent to send him to the program was wasted. All because he was stuck on "being right" and lacked the courage to open himself up to others. As he left, the facilitators' private prognosis was eventual derailment.

Hazard 45: Rigid Adherence to Outdated Policies and Procedures

In some organizations the need for rightness is reinforced by basing rewards and recognition on rigid compliance with established policies and procedures. This can lead to the development of what have been described as "compulsive managers" who base their concept of rightness by blindly adhering to guidelines and procedures that no longer fit (Furnham 2010, 47). This is another case of the need to let go of the old to be relevant to the future. As illustrated by the example of Alexia, derailment awaits those

10. Derailment by the Need to Be Right   89

who are unable to drop blind adherence to policies that no longer make sense.

Coming Off the Tracks by the Compulsive Need to Hold on to What Worked in the Past

Alexia was a human resources vice president who came up through the staffing and recruiting route. She was employed by a large industrial firm that worked from a now proven invalid paradigm that the salespeople who sold their sophisticated equipment had to have both an engineering degree and a high grade point average. They recruited directly from the campus and, as a college recruiter, Alexia had the difficult job of convincing technically trained, high achieving new grads that their future was in selling.

College recruiting is a numbers game and it cost her firm both time and money to fly college seniors to their headquarters and tie up managers in the interviewing process. At the time she earned her spurs on the college recruiting circuit, engineers were in high demand and deciding who should be invited for further interviews and predicting which ones would actually accept an offer were important choices.

Alexia was measured by three ratios: interview to visit (the number of people she interviewed and those who visited her firm's headquarters); visit to offer (the ratio of those who visited to those who actually received an offer); and offer to acceptance (the number who accepted offers compared to those who received them). The last two were the most important and, of all the firm's recruiters, her numbers were clearly the best. She made quick, accurate, organizationally beneficial individual decisions and was rewarded by promotion to corporate staffing manager and eventually to the position of human resources vice president for a large, autonomous division.

Her new division was the largest recipient of new college graduate, engineering-trained sales representatives. Upon arrival she found that the division had retained a consulting company to do an evaluation of the actual skills and duties of salespeople. The study was triggered by a very high turnover rate. Too many engineers with high grade point averages were quitting and accepting positions elsewhere. The consultants recommended that the selection criteria should change and better results and lower turnover could be achieved by dropping the requirement for an engineering degree and, instead, seeking selling skills. Alexia's staff and sales management strongly agreed but Alexia vetoed the recommendation, insisting that she had direct experience, corporate standards required an engineering degree, and that she was right in conceptualizing the problem as simply one of training, not of job specifications. The result was that turnover continued to go up and Alexia's credibility went the other direction.

Her first year was an accelerating downward spiral and she didn't get another. In addition to the poor decision on the requirement for engineering degrees, she ignored the advice of her labor relations staff, followed obsolete corporate guidelines, and didn't compromise over a minor wage dispute, instead choosing to negotiate herself and causing a short, but costly strike. She, in an attempt to save money, terminated her organization development staff despite the fact that the line managers they served saw them as the most valued and trusted component of her HR organization. Her boss, a new general manager appointed by the board of directors to change the procedure bound culture, assessed her as stubborn, not a team player, and unable to gain the respect and confidence of her peers. Her annual performance review was an exit interview.

Hazard 46: Inability to Tolerate the Vulnerability of Accessing Others for Help

The Necessary Combination of Wisdom and Courage

Alexia's derailment serves as an example that individual decision making, while often rewarded at lower levels, can cause derailment toward the top of the organizational pyramid. What Alexia needed was the wisdom to know that in the volatile, complex and uncertain world of organizational leadership no one person has all the answers. After working with Alexia, it became clear that she was insecure in her new role and, rather than ask for help and appear vulnerable, she over-compensated by tenaciously clinging to her own "rightness," and the invulnerability of corporate policy.

The other thing Alexia needed was courage. With her prior conditioning in a rules-oriented culture, difficult though it may have been, she needed to let go of her dependence on invalid procedures and drop her "need to be right" façade. This required flexibility, the willingness to access others, and the openness to value their opinions. Successful leaders have learned that making unilateral decisions is not a sign of strength, and accessing others is not a sign of weakness. The fundamental question wise leaders ask themselves is, "How do I know what I don't know, and how can I find

10. Derailment by the Need to Be Right

out?" The answer always lies with other people and leaders who don't find and access them, face the prospect of derailment.

Perspective and Advice

- The higher one resides in the organizational hierarchy, the more necessary it is to back away from non-collaborative, individual decision making and seek the advice and perspective of others. It's a bit of a bait-and-switch style because rapid individual decisions are rewarded at lower levels but often result in derailment at the top.
- In order to minimize the chances of derailment two powerful, and often difficult to develop, attributes are necessary. The first is the wisdom to know there are things you don't know. The second is the courage to drop the veneer of invulnerability and personal "rightness" and open yourself up to others.
- Personal and organizational learning are the basic components of individual and business survival in our volatile global environment. Refusal to let go of a façade of "rightness" for fear of vulnerability blocks learning and growth. Leaders who are stuck on only their way of conceptualizing problems and organizing solutions risk organizational stagnation. In both the individual and organizational context, derailment is a predictable outcome.
- If you are being promoted into a leadership role that is more complex in scope and scale from your former position, know that what you did to get that promotion is not what you need to do to succeed in your new position. Don't get stuck in defensive "rightness" or stubborn reliance on outdated procedures. Find ways to access others, understand their perspective, and cultivate the wisdom and power of collaboration.
- If you are involved in leadership selection, beware of picking a leader based solely on a track record of making rapid, procedurally compliant past decisions. You are picking someone to play in another, much more complex and ambiguous league. Seek out those with the potential to access others and the belief in the synergistic power of teamwork and collaboration. Above all beware of the toxic consequences of combining arrogance, ego, and blind adherence to self-assessed rightness. Remember the fates of Custer and Napoleon.

11. Derailment by the Need to Be Nasty

> "You don't lead by hitting people over the head—that's assault, not leadership." —*Dwight David Eisenhower*

An abrasive, intimidating, bullying style was the most frequent reason for leadership derailment in The Center for Creative Leadership's initial research over 30 years ago (McCall and Lombardo 1983) and it remains at the top of the pyramid today. Nasty leaders inevitably derail but, along the way, they inflict heavy damage to both organizational effectiveness and individual creativity. The saga of Nasty John provides insight into the dynamics of this widespread dysfunctional style.

Hazard 47: An Abrasive, Intimidating Style

Nasty John and the Dynamics of a Derailment

I'm usually reluctant to take on an executive coaching client when his boss has predetermined the problem and has a specific solution in mind. I'm even more wary when the boss wants the employee "fixed." In most cases the diagnosis follows the classic pattern of "He's good technically but he has interpersonal problems. I need you to improve his people skills." Joint diagnosis and action planning in collaboration with the client always is more effective than working within the constraints of the boss's external prescription, but against my better judgment I eventually accepted the assignment. It didn't end well but serves as an excellent illustration of the dynamics of derailment by nastiness.

John was a marketing executive in the pharmaceutical industry and, like many in that field, his company was part of the acquisition food chain

11. Derailment by the Need to Be Nasty

of smaller fish being swallowed by larger fish that, in turn, were gobbled up by even bigger fish. He was a scarred veteran of three mergers and managed to survive by making hard decisions regarding post-merger layoffs and consolidated organizational structures. A common descriptive term used was that he was "a tough SOB." His self-description was "brutally honest." However, the longer I worked with him the clearer it became that he enjoyed the brutality more than the honesty.

As is the case with many nasty executives, frequent organizational and job changes tended to mask his fundamental problem. In John's case, his abrasive and bullying style was actually reinforced by his reputation as a useful post-acquisition tough guy. Similar to conditions that cause the inevitable outings of other nasties, a period of stability, a new boss, and an organizational culture that valued respect for others exposed his destructive style.

The pace of mergers slowed dramatically and John was given a new role leading a group of talented, long-term, product managers charged with marketing sophisticated, highly competitive products. The product managers were, themselves, highly marketable; any one of them could go to a competitor and secure a higher paying job. That is exactly what happened when, two months into John's regime, three left. Another derailment reality for nasties is that abrasive "tough guys" can get away with it with some people, some of the time, in some organizational contexts, but it will eventually catch up with them. In John's situation, terminations from three valuable employees plus complaints from his peers and subordinates quickly got the attention of his firm's top executives.

Abused children, when they grow up, tend to abuse their own children and that parallelism held true with John. His first boss was abrasive and extremely intimidating but John survived and learned. When his boss was fired, John took his place and emulated his style. For new, impressionable employees, working for a nasty boss can be a seductive experience. The long-term toxicity of intimidation and abrasion can be masked by the illusion of power and control. Unless careful, impressionable subordinates can choose a very damaging role model.

Through frequent job changes, shifting organizational cultures and short-term, "make tough decisions and fix it" assignments, John stayed one step ahead of facing the damaging consequences of his nastiness. It was only during a period of stability that the chickens had the time and space to eventually come home to roost and John finally derailed.

Helping John gain insight into the negative consequences of his style proved to be a hopeless task. His defensive attack-and-intimidate style sometimes materialized when he was working with me and, increasingly, with his new boss. We also discovered that he was cloning a key subordinate who was developing the next generation of nasty skills. The critical incident that led to Nasty John's demise occurred when he barged into a subordinate's closed door session with a top manager, dressed down the subordinate, and demanded the meeting stop. The top manager resided higher in the totem pole than John's boss and his intervention ended John's career and, mercifully, my own frustrating coaching engagement.

Hazard 48: Adopting a Nasty Boss as a Role Model

Lessons from Nasty John's Journey to Derailment

John's saga demonstrated five truths concerning the development and eventual demise of nasty leaders:

- An abrasive, nasty style begins early in a leader's career, and is often learned from a nasty role model.
- Unless dealt with and corrected early on, their style becomes increasingly difficult to change.
- Latent nastiness is often reinforced by short assignments that put a premium on "toughness."
- Nasty leaders can survive and avoid detection by frequent changes in assignments.
- They inevitably get found out and that almost always leads to derailment.

Why Nasty Leaders Eventually Derail

Nasty leaders are destined to derail for three reasons. First, they are unable to nurture work joy, spontaneity, creativity, and productivity in their employees. Employees who work for nasty leaders tend to keep their heads down, hunker down in the trenches and not take reasonable risks. Secondly, their peers don't trust them and are wary of any level of interpersonal interaction. This results in the nasty leader feeling isolated and paranoid, further stimulating his dysfunctional abrasiveness. Finally, regardless of their talents, the bosses of nasty leaders grow weary of responding to complaints, losing good people, and treading on eggs when attempting to provide developmental feedback.

Causes of the Need to Be Nasty

Since nasty leaders are so widespread and frustrating to help, their peers, bosses, and subordinates tend to be curious about what makes them that way; why they have a need to be nasty. Curiosity is understandable, probing and attempting to intervene in root causes, as will be illustrated in the case of Janice and Bubba, is not. Amateur diagnosis and intervention is dangerous, unethical, and potentially career ending. The reason is that most experts connect the root cause of nastiness to early childhood issues and, unless you are a trained and licensed therapist, attempting to intervene takes you out of your depth and is playing with fire. A good rule when dealing with nasties is to descriptively deal with the effects of dysfunctional behavior but never get seduced into attempting to diagnose or deal with root causes. Analytical psychologist Harry Levinson (2006) articulates the complexity and magnitude of the root cause when he describes the "abrasive personality" as an insatiable need for perfection combined with a basic lack of self esteem:

> Needing to see himself as extraordinary, he acts sometimes as if he were a privileged person—indeed, as if he had a right to be different or even inconsiderate. At times he sees others as mere devices for his self-aggrandizement, existing as extensions of himself, rather than as full-fledged, unique adults with their own wishes, desires, and aspirations. To inflate his always low sense of self-worth, he competes intensely for attention, affection, and applause. At the same time, he seems to expect others to accept his word, decision, or logic just because it is his. When disappointed in these expectations, he becomes enraged [103].

Alfred Adler, the psychiatrist who developed the concept of the inferiority complex, again harkens back to early developmental issues that lead to adult nastiness. He concludes that the inferiority complex arises from a universal infantile feeling of helplessness and sees it as a form of overcompensation that leads to aggression. (Hoffman 1994). Leadership researcher, Adrian Furnham (2010 15) specifically relates nasty leadership to early developmental trauma when he summarizes studies that compare "healthy self esteem" with "destructive narcissism." The cause is a traumatic childhood leading to the development of "arrogant, self-absorbed, narcissistic leaders."

Hazard 49: Attempting to Fix the Root Motivational Drive of a Chronic Nasty

The Story of Janice and Bubba: The Folly of Trying to Change an Entrenched Nasty

Janice paid her dues on the rocky path to her first general management job. She accepted tough, challenging assignments without complaining. She put in long hours to the detriment of her personal life. She knew men who worked less hard at easier jobs and made more money but she never played the gender discrimination card. Her sacrifices eventually paid off. She was promoted to general manager of a specialized manufacturing division. She was the first woman to hold this position, and since her company finally got the message regarding the legal—they still haven't digested the moral—obligation of equal pay for equal work, she received a substantial salary increase and a generous stock option.

Her division assembled and built computer memory devices that were integrated into her own firm's mainframes and also custom built products for other companies. Although not part of the division's technical aristocracy, packaging, shipping, receiving, and managing the constant ebb and flow of components and completed devices was an important and busy activity. The person who ran this operation was Bubba, an unrepentant nasty.

In military terms, Bubba was a Mustang—someone who came up through the ranks and was promoted to officer without going through the traditional educational or social hoops. Bubba's colleagues were all degreed engineers and many also had MBAs. But for the influence of his football coach, Bubba wouldn't have made it through high school. He felt out of place which led to anger, which further fueled his fundamental nastiness.

Bubba was a terror, but an effective terror. Components and products were unerringly packaged, shipped, received and accounted for. The division paid a steep price for this efficiency in terms of high turnover, low morale, and formal grievances from Bubba's group. The former general manager was simply afraid to confront Bubba and was content to reap the efficiency and pay the price. Janice wasn't. Never one to back away from a challenge, she resolved to "fix" Bubba. Her misguided method was making Bubba take a battery of personality tests, share the results, and help him gain insight and change his nasty behavioral pattern.

Her human resources director was young, inexperienced, and intrigued with psychological personality tests. He had taken a couple of classes in psychology in conjunction with his degree in business administration, but was by no means qualified to purchase, administer, or interpret the battery of tests he and Janice forced on Bubba.

Viewed through the eyes of a qualified and licensed professional, the results were quite intriguing. Much of Bubba's ingrained nastiness seemed to result from self esteem issues. Even making a slight dent in his behavior, let alone "fixing" him, would have required a skilled therapist, a significant amount of time, and Bubba's sincere motivation to change. When they jointly sat down with Bubba, the HR director and Janice were over their heads ethically, professionally, and legally.

From the company's standpoint the meeting was a disaster. Bubba mobilized his nasty skills, angrily arguing the results and engaging his well-practiced powers of intimidation to challenge their credentials and right to administer and interpret the tests in the first place. Neither Janice, nor her HR director, really understood the methodology and normative base of the tests or how to use the results to facilitate insight and behavioral change and were stymied by Bubba's nasty response. The meeting ended with Bubba walking out and slamming the door.

Nasty though he was, Bubba didn't get where he was by stupidity. He engaged a lawyer and together they produced a history of positive performance appraisals and documents outlining the credentials necessary to purchase, administer, and interpret the psychological tests he was given. The company didn't have a chance. They opened the corporate wallet and paid what it took to make it go away.

Bubba was three years from retirement and what it took to make both "it" and him go away was bridging the gap and immediately giving him full retirement benefits, paying the fee for his attorney, and a hefty personal cash settlement. Janice got off relatively easily. She received a stern warning and learned two valuable lessons. The first was the futility of attempting to change the basic motivation of a chronic nasty. The second was to not be lead astray by the unrealistic aspirations of human resource officials. The human resource director, who unfortunately worked in my chain of command, didn't fare so well. He lost his job.

A Good Boss–Bad Boss Trait Comparison

A simple comparative exercise can validate the ubiquity of nasty leader behavioral traits. It can be done individually as a frame of reference for reflection, or as a part of a group exercise to stimulate discussion. All that's needed is a blank sheet of paper, a pen, and a few minutes of reflective time.

The first step is to think of the very best boss you ever had. Take a minute to get a fix on what that person actually did to earn that honor. Then prioritize those traits on one side of the paper. Turn the paper over and think of the very worse boss you ever worked for and make another list. This exercise has been used with groups in organizations of all kinds during the past thirty years and, if your answers are similar to theirs, your "good boss" list had words like "empowering," "helpful," and "fair." Bad boss lists are usually longer and have polar opposite descriptors such as "unfair," "intimidating," "aggressive," and "uncaring"—all traits of nasty bosses.

Perspective and Advice

- If you have a nasty working for you, unless you are a trained therapist, know that delving too deeply into psychoanalytic theory and practice is not the way to help nasty employees. Based on my experience and trained therapists' advice, here are three straightforward tips: (1) Deal with the problem early in the nasty's career by engaging in straight talk based on observed behavior and potential consequences; (2) Be patient, as continual reinforcement of the basic message is necessary; (3) Use more praise than blame—nasty managers are, deep down, striving for affirmation; (4) If you are not making progress and still feel that saving the nasty is worth the time and money involved, insist on external therapeutic help.
- If you receive feedback that your behavior is seen as overly aggressive, abrasive, or intimidating, don't blow it off. Although it will feel difficult, generate the courage to look in the mirror and don't back away from what you see. Chances are you are seen as a valuable contributor since, despite the negative perceptions of others, you still have your job. Know that, unless you make some fundamental changes in your style, you probably won't have that job long term.
- Find a helper and a truth teller. It can be one person with both attributes, or two different individuals. A truth teller is someone you trust with the visibility and willingness to tell you the truth

about the impact of your behavior on others. A helper is a person with the skills to coach and help you change.
- Don't be reluctant to seek external, professional help. Even if you have to pay for it yourself, working with a competent therapist may be the only way to save your career.

12. Derailment by the Need to Be Busy

> "I was surprised that others didn't text during that client meeting."—*Exit interview comment by a manager derailed for inappropriate busyness*

The need to be—or, in some cases, appear to be—busy manifests itself differently by organizational level. Many mid-level managers succumb to career-limiting multitasking mania. Leaders toward the top of organizations face a different busyness hazard, what management theorist George Odiorne (1974) describes as an "activity trap." This occurs when a leader becomes so focused on an individual activity she loses track of its context and ultimate purpose while ignoring other important issues.

Hazard 50: Confusing Busyness and Multitasking with Productivity

The Anatomy of a Multitasking Derailment

As illustrated by Faith's derailment, busyness-obsessed middle managers may not actually lose their jobs but they can be removed from the fast track and their ascension to the top blocked. I ran into Faith while working in a large financial services firm. She was a newly minted MBA from a "prestigious" university and worked in a business lending unit that had an emphasis on making large loans to credit-worthy clients and providing excellent customer service. Professional restraint and a slight aura of controlled stuffiness characterized the unit's culture. Frenzied activity was not congruent with the unwritten organizational norms but Faith did not get the message.

During her first six months, which in that organization constituted a formal probationary period, she made several busyness-denominated, counter-cultural, career-limiting moves. She answered her phone, went through her inbox, texted, and responded to email during one-on-one sessions with those she felt were below her in the hierarchy. When interacting with her peers or bosses, she displayed a terse, nervous impatience, giving the impression that she had more important things to do than to meet with them. The event that finally took her off the fast track and plateaued her career was when she continually texted during an important client meeting with her boss and other executives.

MBAs from "prestigious" schools are expensive to hire and, in Faith's company, put on an accelerated development plan. Thus, her derailment and eventual resignation had more than normal top management visibility. Her exit interview provided them with three insights concerning the dynamics of derailment by the need to be busy. First, she was blindsided by a clash of cultures and impaired by her own naïveté. She thought her multitasking busyness would impress her bosses, not alienate them. Secondly, unlike her older colleagues and management, she grew up with a smart phone in her hand and was conditioned by the ubiquity of social media. She saw nothing wrong with texting during a client meeting and, in fact, was "surprised" that the other attendees didn't do the same. Lastly, she equated productivity with multitasking. She had no experience with face-to-face dialogue and reflective communication. Even when with friends, she much preferred texting and looking at her phone than articulating words and making eye contact.

Hazard 51: Lack of Interpersonal Competence

Efficiency, Multitasking and What It Really Takes to Succeed

Although multitasking may seem efficient and time saving, there is an increasing stream of research that concludes the opposite. Computers may be able to switch from task to task and back again without losing a beat, but the human brain just doesn't work that way. People who focus on one task at a time are actually inclined to be more efficient than those who multitask (Rubinstein, Meyer, and Evans 2001). Efficiency is but one, somewhat narrow and mechanistic, measure of what it takes to thrive and grow in hierarchal organizations. Interpersonal competence—skills such as active listening, empathy, and self-awareness—are the necessary currency of the realm. Too many technology savvy, social media–conditioned young employees use multitasking to mask their interpersonal faults and they do so at the risk of limiting their careers.

Hazard 52: Phony Busyness

The Fallacy of Faking It

Some upward-striving newly minted managers attempt to impress organizational leaders with an artificial image of their busyness. They naïvely think that busyness equates to productivity and that by faking it, their bosses will notice them. Whenever I notice this behavior I'm reminded of a scene in the first act of the play based on a book by Mead (1952), *How to Succeed in Business Without Really Trying: The Dastard's Guide to Fame and Fortune*. In the play, the central character, J. Pierrepont Finch, arrives early, clutters his desk, pulls several feet of tape from his adding machine, and leans back in his chair with his tie askew and a glazed look in his eyes. He waits for the company president to arrive in order to create the impression that he worked all night. The ruse worked in the play but it falls flat in real life. Most senior managers and organizational leaders know the difference between reality and fiction and are offended by artificial busyness.

Employees attempting to influence their bosses by creating artificial situations designed to demonstrate their busyness face dual hazards. They waste a lot of energy concocting an image that is easily debunked and they demonstrate a belief in the fallacy that frenzied activity has a connection with real, authentic, work. In both cases they face a substantial risk of career limitation or actual job loss.

Hazard 53: Activity Traps

Activity traps are fodder for the derailment of senior organizational leaders. They are particularly dangerous because they can affect not only the performance of an individual, but of an entire organization. They often take the form of self-perceived burdensome duties that are a distraction to more substantial concerns.

The Dual Danger of Activity Traps

In terms of executive derailment, activity traps have two contradictory dimensions. The first is an irrational focus on only one issue along with an inordinate channeling of energy toward dealing with it at the exclusion of other equal or more important issues. The second is that the problem becomes central to the executive's identity and if solved, paradoxically reduces her sense of purpose.

In my research on the effects of downsizing on organizational survivors (Noer, 2009), I encountered leaders who were trapped in the jaws of an obsession with cost cutting and headcount reduction. This activity trap became so time consuming and distracting that it eclipsed any proactive strategy to grow the business, develop new products, or improve profitability.

Hazard 54: Cost-Cutting Mania

The Negative Consequence of Joe's Staff Reduction Vendetta

Joe was the chief operating officer for a computer manufacturing firm. With the advent of personal computers, his branch of the mainframe business hit the skids. Commercial orders dried up and government and military systems procurement slowed. His corporation faced the classic doomsday triangle: too many people, too few orders, and too many fixed expenses.

Joe came up through the engineering ranks and always had an aversion to administrative staff people. This included personnel from human resources, legal, advertising, public relations, planning, security, facilities, and most accountants. Even in boom times, he just couldn't grasp their value. He had his way. During the first round of layoffs, some of these functions were eliminated and the remainder were radically cut. The layoffs didn't stop with staff employees. Four more rounds took place in the next year. Employees in all disciplines and all locations were cut.

In addition to not liking staff functions, Joe had another trait. Throughout his career he was a vigorous and driven cost cutter. He took the size of the corporation's general and administrative expenses as a personal insult and was ruthless in budget slashing. Hard times only accelerated his mania for expense reduction. As the firm's financial condition continued to erode, Joe crossed an important paradigmatic line: he measured his self-worth, not by improving profitability, but only with cutting costs and reducing headcount. In classic activity trap fashion, his self esteem was grounded in one set of activities to the exclusion of others.

Things did turn around but Joe didn't. Two large orders—one from the U.S. government and the other from the Middle East—stabilized cash flow and an acquisition introduced a new and profitable product line. The company had downsized so much that it needed to resume recruiting while concurrently working to restore the morale and commitment of those who survived the layoffs. Joe couldn't drop his cost-cutting activity trap. In an all-staff employee communication where the CEO wanted to rally the troops around the new orders and the return to profitability, Joe both embarrassed and angered him by publicly disputing his decision to resume hiring. He next unsuccessfully attempted to cut the funding of a series of survivor revitalization workshops recommended by a board member and sponsored by the CEO. That was the last straw. Because of his obsession with cost cutting and his inability to let go and focus on growing the business, he was asked to resign.

Although Joe's derailment was based on cost cutting, career-ending activity traps can take many forms. They can be an unproductive and distracting effort to turn around a poor product, propping up a terminally dysfunctional organizational unit, or relentlessly pursuing an untested and unmarketable technology.

Hazard 55: An Obsession for Busyness

Working Hard on the Wrong Things: A Recipe for Derailment

Lars was raised on a small farm on the rich bottom lands of the Minnesota River in Southern Minnesota. His real name was Maynard Larson, but he hated Maynard and only answered to it when his stern, controlling father used it. Although small by Minnesota standards, the farm did well except in those years when the river flooded; then it produced mostly mud. Lars lost his mother when he was four and he and his older brother worked the land under the not-so-benevolent dictatorship of his father.

His father, a second generation Swede, was functionally illiterate; he only made it through third grade before his father, an itinerant preacher,

12. Derailment by the Need to Be Busy

moved on to still another Swedish-speaking community. Lars's father overcame his lack of education and embarrassment over his inability to read or write by relentless hard work and what Minnesotans call "stubborn Swede" will power. He ruled the farm through rigorous discipline and liberal application of his leather belt on the backsides of his sons. The three biggest sins for Lars and his brother were missing one day of school, not attending every early Sunday service in their local Lutheran Church and idleness—not being busy on the farm. Of the three, idleness was considered, by far, the most sinful.

Lars grew up smart, big and strong and was offered a football scholarship to a Lutheran-affiliated college in Southern Minnesota. His older brother had no interest in college and stayed on the farm. His father, reluctantly approved Lars's plans for college, but only with his promise to spend weekends, summers, and holidays working at the farm.

Lars's leather belt–conditioned, ingrained reverence for busyness served him well in college. Between academics, football, and serving his time at the farm, there was no room in his life for idleness or engaging in the developmental pleasures of college social life. During his junior year, his father's life-long smoking addiction caught up with him. He lasted almost a year, but during Lars's senior year, the cancer won. By the time he graduated, his father had been buried, the farm had been sold, and his brother had moved to South Dakota to be with his girlfriend. Lars graduated in the top ten percent of his class and walked away from college with a degree in psychology, no close family, and a burning need to find a place to lose himself in busyness.

He found that place in the HR department of a rapidly growing computer company. His initial role involved recruiting electrical engineers and computer programmers. It was as much a sales job as a recruiting job because it was a very tight labor market and the company could offer growth but not competitive salaries. Lars thrived. He was a relentless recruiter and a persuasive salesman. He worked long hours, weekends, and when out of town on college recruiting trips, where he never socialized over drinks with his colleagues, just returned to his hotel room and kept working.

His hard work and perpetual busyness paid off and he was promoted to a managerial role, directing HR, as well as purchasing and facilities for a newly opened rural manufacturing assembly plant. One of the reasons for his selection was that the plant was located in a small town not far from the farm where he grew up and it was assumed that he would have empathy and be able to easily relate to the workforce. It was a bad assumption. Empathy and social skills were never components of his cultural conditioning.

The reason his company started an assembly plant in rural Minnesota was that it gave them access to a large labor pool that had a good work ethic, would not be prone to union activity, would work for relatively low wages, and would be grateful for jobs with fringe benefits. Many of the assembly workers were farm wives, working to supplement their family incomes. Lars and his managerial colleagues were big fish in a small pond—the plant quickly became the largest employer in the county. As big fish, they were expected, both by their company and local officials, to be visible and active participants in community affairs.

Hints of Lars's eventual derailment began with his refusal to waste time schmoozing with small town politicians, citizen groups, and local affiliates of national service clubs. He once, at the orders of the plant manager, accepted an invitation to speak at the Elks club, but brought his laptop, worked over dinner and, even though he had a half hour, gave only a five-minute, factually accurate, but immensely boring speech. He didn't stay for questions because he said he had to get back to work.

At work, the curse of the childhood leather belt played out. This was his first supervisory job and he did unto his employees what his father had done onto him: punished them for even giving the appearance of not being busy. Tongue lashings—often in public—unfair performance evaluations, and weekend make-work assignments were his leather belt.

As the top HR officer, he carried his rigid and judgmental work ethic into the workforce. One event which, when added to his poor reputation in the community, helped accelerate his downward slide toward derailment, occurred because he noticed that one carpool of assemblers arrived a half hour late for work. It was a dark February morning and the carpool driver had to combat a Minnesota winter storm while picking up women from distant locations. The plant manager was out of town and Lars was the senior manager in residence that day. He ordered the supervisor of the women in the car pool to keep them an hour later than normal quitting time—a half hour to make up for their lateness and another half hour to teach them a lesson. There were several negative results. Kids didn't get picked up from school and farm chores went undone. A formal grievance was filed because overtime wasn't paid and a union representative appeared at the plant entrance. An angry group of male farmers came to the building and confronted the plant manager.

Lars didn't last a year. When the hammer fell he was surprised. His early conditioning blinded him to differentiating between looking busy and doing meaningful work. His real work was building and maintaining positive community relationships and developing a productive workforce that resisted unionization. His obsession with looking busy resulted from early developmental conditioning that didn't fit the reality of organizational demands and, without a substantial investment in time, money, and outside help, would have been very difficult to correct.

Hazard 56: Colluding to Project an Artificial Image of Productive Work

A different form of obsession occurs when leaders and managers allow the image of busyness to eclipse the reality of authentic work. A common practice is to fake busyness to impress the boss. Too often, the boss colludes in the process by pretending to be impressed by the fakery. The process becomes even more counterproductive when allowed to climb the hierarchical ladder with many levels colluding by building an artificial image of productivity. Entire organizational units can become obsessed with looking busy without actually accomplishing meaningful work. I have, most often, observed this form of collective fakery in highly bureaucratized organizations with fixed external funding and isolated, uninvolved top management. The cycle is broken when someone—almost always an outsider, an external new hire, or a transplant from a different part of the organization—enters the system, bursts the balloon of collusion and insists on meaningful work. Those who can't make the adjustment and continue to play the game are vulnerable to derailment.

Perspective and Advice

- If you are a manager and think that multitasking busyness and frenzied activity will improve your promotional potential, think again. Busyness does not equate to productivity and the image you create will be that of a shallow, self-absorbed manager who needs to change to remain on the high-potential list.
- If you are new to the world of business, know that social media

addiction will derail you. Be smart and keep your smart phone under wraps. Texting while interacting with others may be normal on the street, in a restaurant, or the classroom, but not during business meetings or one-on-one sessions with your co-workers. Active listening, eye contact, and the ability to form empathetic authentic, non-device assisted relationships are what will increase your promotional chances and avoid derailment by cell phone.
- Don't become trapped in the erroneous belief that multitasking will increase efficiency and impress your boss. The human brain is not a computer and multitasking actually hinders efficiency. Excessive multitasking will, indeed, get you noticed, but for the wrong reasons. Organizational leaders want people who can focus, appear calm, and have time to authentically connect with other people.
- Activity traps are hazardous to the employment continuity of senior managers. If you find yourself immersed to the point of compulsion with a single issue or a narrow recurring list of tasks, you are caught in the derailment jaws of an activity trap. Ask for feedback from your colleagues, boss, or staff. Let them help you back off, find a broader and more organizationally relevant base for your self esteem and identity. Painful though it may be, escaping the grip of an activity trap will make you a more relevant leader and reduce the odds of derailment.
- If you work for someone whose obsession with busyness is blocking their effectiveness and creating problems for you, you can either try to help her, transfer to another organization, or stand aside and, painful though it may be, suck it up and wait for her to derail. Unfortunately, without time and access to professional external resources, the helping option will prove difficult.
- If you are tempted to fake busyness to impress the boss, think again. It's an illusionary process and, even if the boss buys in and colludes with your fakery, it is a dead end street. Productivity won't improve and the game will eventually come to an end.

PART V
WARPED PERCEPTIONS

The common thread of the three derailment risks in this section is that they are formed by distorted perceptions and warped mental models. Those who derail by gunnysack are trapped by repressed and distorted feelings of anger and paranoia. Derailment by fantasy involves head-in-the-sand reliance on outdated mental models and delusional optimism. Leaders who come off the track because of cross-cultural blindness are unable to visualize differences in cultural values and are perceptually stuck in their own cultural norms.

Part V Chapter Summary

The Three Categories of Warped Perception Risks and How to Navigate Them

Derailment Risks	*What to Do About Them*
Chapter 13: Gunnysacking: Accumulating a heavy burden of unvented feelings, emotions, and frustrations.	Keep your gunnysack light by continually externalizing its contents. Don't allow it to get too heavy and overwhelm you.
Chapter 14: Fantasy: Judgments and actions warped by false and unrealistic perceptions.	Cultivate healthy self-doubt and have the courage to engage in regular reality checks by accessing others.
Chapter 15: Cross-Cultural Blindness: Inability to visualize the different ways country and regional cultures shape employee values and motivation.	Learn the basic concepts of cross-cultural research and apply them to your leadership practice.

13. Derailment by Gunnysack

> "Those self-serving SOBs in sales have always had it in for me." —*Comment by a derailed, gunnysack-laden manager*

Gunnysacking is a term for accumulating and storing hurt feelings, jealousies, unresolved conflicts and anger. Imagine the burden of carrying around a gunnysack filled with these heavy, energy-draining, judgment-distorting feelings and emotions. We all carry gunnysacks but most healthy people find ways to keep theirs relatively empty by externalizing their disabling emotional baggage. Others allow the accumulated weight of their gunnysack to either chronically distort their perceptions and behavior or, in response to a relatively minor triggering event, suddenly dump the entire contents in a jolting emotional outburst. In both cases the result can be derailment.

Hazard 57: Bottling Up Unresolved Emotions Until They Explode

Hierarchical organizations are fertile breeding grounds for the powerful, unresolved emotions that accumulate—sometimes for years—in metaphorical gunnysacks. Missed promotions, interdepartmental rivalries, functional conflicts, in-group out-group tensions, and abusive bosses are all fuel for gunnysacking. A compounding factor is that many organizations have strong norms against displaying feelings and emotions in the work place and many employees don't seek external relief. With no outlet, energy, creativity, and productivity suffer while employees stagger through the work week, burdened by heavy gunnysacks. In tough economic times, gunnysack-toting employees are often among the first to lose their jobs.

13. Derailment by Gunnysack

Others derail themselves by allowing a single triggering incident to open the floodgates and release years of frustration in a career-limiting torrent of repressed emotions. That's what happened to Dan.

The Straw That Derailed the Camel: A Gunnysacking Case Study

Small, seemingly inconsequential acts can serve as the proverbial "straw that broke the camel's back." In this case it wasn't a camel; it was a seasoned manager and it wasn't a straw; it was a light-hearted comment by a sales executive. I conducted an exit interview and assisted with the post-mortem analysis of Dan, an accounting manager who, I was told, "blew up" in a meeting. He was still hot when I talked to him, blaming the "self-serving SOBs in sales" who "had it in for him" for his demise. He was promptly shunted off into a non-supervisory dead end job, and, after a 15-year, relatively successful career, eventually resigned and accepted a much lower-level job.

Early in his career Dan crossed paths with a cynical and ruthless sales manager. He was attempting to enforce compliance with a business expense policy but the manager, who occupied a higher perch on the corporate totem pole, made it a personal issue, belittling him in a public meeting, challenging his professionalism, and accusing him of supervising the "sales prevention" department. In the context of a 15-year career, most employees, if they remembered it at all, would interpret it as a very minor event. Dan, who wasn't blessed with an overabundance of self esteem and compensated for it with a chronic case of mild paranoia, didn't take it that way. It opened up an ever expanding gunnysack where, over the years, he accumulated a heavy burden of often inaccurate and untested grievances and slights against the sales function in general and one department in particular.

During a budget meeting attended by senior management from both the sales and accounting functions, a high-level sales executive jokingly used the triggering phrase "sales prevention department" when describing the credit function, one of several that reported to Dan. He lost it. The camel's back was broken and so, ultimately, was Dan's career. In a profanity-laden rant, he spewed forth years of accumulated emotional baggage. When his gunnysack was finally empty, his boss was mortified, the sales executive was furious, and the HR department was notified that Dan didn't possess the emotional stability to remain in a management role.

Despite his issues with self esteem, his tendency to take too many innocuous things personally, and a mindset that other functions were not to be completely trusted, Dan, although no superstar, wasn't a bad manager. In some ways, these traits complimented his role. What derailed Dan was his inability to reduce the stultifying burden of his gunnysack.

The accumulated weight of gunnysacks can be reduced by the process of externalization. This involves sharing the contents with someone else: talking about it. It can be a friend, a boss, a significant other or a helping professional. Sharing the burden with a trusted "other" can work magic. All managers carry gunnysacks. Those who are wise find ways to keep them light by continual externalization. Those who don't risk derailment. That can either happen through eroded performance resulting from being ground down over time, or as happed with Dan, by a violent emotional outburst.

Hazard 58: Allowing Repressed Emotions to Permanently Damage Perceptions

Richard Nixon's Perpetually Heavy Gunnysack

Perhaps the best public example of derailment fostered by the cumulative effect of carrying a heavy gunnysack was President Richard Nixon's resignation in 1974. The Watergate break-in and its cover up were the result of behavior stimulated by the weight of long-standing, chronically distorted perceptions. In *All the President's Men*, Woodward and Bernstein (1974) provided clues that Nixon's private behavior was fueled by the weight of a gunnysack filled with mistrust, secretiveness, and paranoia. Weiner (2015, 5) captures the toxic effect of that gunnysack, "A darker spirit animated him—malevolent and violent, driven by anger and an insatiable appetite for revenge." He carried that crippling weight for a long time. After losing the 1962 California gubernatorial election he provided another clue to his underlying paranoia with his defensive, self-pitying, farewell statement, "You won't have Dick Nixon to kick around anymore." Ten years earlier, when responding to allegations of misusing campaign funds, he again reverted to maudlin deflection with his "Checkers" speech, using the gift of a Cocker Spaniel to elicit sympathy and mask the true contents of his gunnysack.

13. Derailment by Gunnysack

Derailment by gunnysack does not always involve, as in the example of Dan, a single episode where coworkers were figuratively beaten about the head with a heavy, unopened gunnysack before it was dramatically opened and the contents scattered about the room. Derailment can result from a series of smaller incidents cumulatively resulting in a career coming off the tracks. There are situations, as in the example of President Nixon, when the gunnysack is never really opened and derailment is caused by warped perspectives that eventually lead to career-limiting behaviors. These are perhaps the most tragic because the underlying emotional wounds are never externalized and remain festering in the dark interior of the gunnysack long after the carrier is derailed.

Revenge by Gunnysack: A "Nerdy Introvert" Strikes Back

Carl was a bright electrical engineer working for a growing firm that made storage devices for computer systems. His high IQ was more than offset by his abysmally low emotional intelligence quotient. His director made the common mistake of promoting him to a managerial role only because of his engineering skills. Soon after his promotion, the number of employee complaints, requests for transfers, and resignations markedly increased. Since the organization was in a chaotic growth mode, his departmental issues were overlooked and he was actually promoted one more time before his gunnysack-motivated behavior finally caught up with him.

I and his new supervisor were tasked to diagnose the problem and try to "help" Carl. What we discovered was that he continually ridiculed and picked on his employees, sending the message that they were stupid, incompetent, and not up to his standards. Worse, he seemed to enjoy putting down people in public. In digging into his background, we found that both in graduate school and as a non-supervisory engineer, he was, as described by a former co-worker, a "nerdy introvert with no real friends," who was "desperate for respect and recognition." While in a non-supervisory role, his path to these ends was to show off his superior skills and intellect while concurrently disparaging those of his peers. In his managerial role, he had a broader podium and a more captive audience.

After several frustrating sessions with Carl it became clear that he had no interest in either seeking professional help for the underlying self esteem issues festering in his gunnysack or in revising his perception that he didn't have a problem to begin with. His boss came to the conclusion that it was a no-win situation. He didn't have the time or patience to help someone who didn't want to be helped. Carl was removed from his managerial role and, since he was exceptionally competent, offered a non-supervisory technical position. Neither his ego, nor his wallet could tolerate a downgrade and the last his boss heard of him was a status report from his outplacement firm indicating that his attitude was putting off potential employers. The developmental loss for Carl was that he didn't learn from his derailment and was doomed to carry his unopened, career-limiting gunnysack with him into the future. He, like President Nixon, allowed the accumulated weight of his gunnysack to cause long-term perceptual distortions.

Group Venting: Opening Multiple Gunnysacks to Recover from Downsizing Trauma

Gunnysacks are sometimes quickly filled with large boulders triggered by traumatic events. The violation of the old psychological employment contract, where employees who stayed out of trouble and performed to standards could keep their jobs until they retired or chose to leave, was a major traumatic event. It was replaced by a new psychological employment contract where employees were costs to be minimized and not long-term assets to be nurtured and developed over a career.

The result of this change was an epidemic of layoff survivor sickness (Noer 1997). Employees who psychologically signed up under the old contract, survived massive layoffs, and found themselves in the midst of the new contract were angry, depressed, and frightened. This was not the kind of a workforce necessary to help organizations rebound and reap the rewards of the cost savings from a reduced payroll. Productivity dropped and profitability projections were missed.

In a highly competitive global economy, many organizations were fielding workforces weighed down by heavy gunnysacks. Some resisted and simply expected employees to "suck it up" and move forward regardless of the burdens they carried. Others were wiser and discovered that an investment in gunnysack emptying would result in substantial returns.

I and some colleagues facilitated a number of successful group venting sessions focused on reducing the weight of productivity-limiting gunnysacks. The first stage involved describing the rocks (anger, fear, anxiety, and violation). Some managers were initially concerned about stimulating "moaning and bitching," but they came to understand that without articulating the contents, the bags would remain full and productivity would remain low. This externalization phase is a facilitated form of emotional catharsis. By sharing the contents of their gunnysacks participants discover that they are not alone and that it is organizationally sanctioned to talk about feelings. If facilitated properly, employees almost always emerge from the externalization stage with lighter gunnysacks, feeling better, and better prepared to move forward. The key is a competent facilitator with the ability to deflect personal attacks and balance participation.

The second stage is a "now that I've vented, what's next" session. Most groups find a way to see the glass as half full and, with lighter bags, return to work with a desire to make things better. The only times they return to work feeling more pessimistic than when they arrived is when top managers minimize the issues or try to talk them out of their feelings. One-time group venting sessions are not a cure-all and much more work is necessary over a longer time to fully restore morale and commitment, but with a skilled facilitator they can reduce the weight of multiple gunnysacks in a surprisingly short time.

Perspective and Advice

- Storing up emotional slights, hurt feelings, and anger can lead to a derailed career and it, most certainly, will lead to lowered productivity, reduced creativity, and unhappiness on and off the job.
- Unrelieved gunnysacking will result in two types of derailing behavior. The first results from letting a triggering incident unleash a torrent of repressed slights, hurt feelings, and anger. That outburst is usually well out of the context of the initiating incident and will be seen by others as indicative of instability and inability to function under pressure. Even if it doesn't result in an immediate dismissal, it will be remembered, limit future options, and can set the stage for a future demotion.
- The second type of derailment by gunnysack involves never lightening the load at all and allowing misperceptions, paranoia, and false attributions to shape behavior. These misperceptions become more apparent to others the higher one raises in organizations and will lead to career derailment along with an unhappy outlook on life.

- The way to prevent derailment by gunnysack is to not let your gunnysack get too heavy. This is done by externalizing emotional blockages and accessing others. We all suffer from hurt feelings, slights, and wounded self esteem. They are inevitable artifacts of organizational life. The trick is to not keep them inside and to talk to someone about them. It doesn't have to be a shrink. It can be a significant other, a friend, or a colleague. Unarticulated negative emotions are toxic, not only to a career, but to a relevant life. Don't ever let your gunnysack get too full or you will pay a heavy price.
- If you find yourself derailed or suspect that it is an imminent prospect, resist the natural urge to deny the existence of an overweight gunnysack. Work to learn from the experience. You can't do this on your own. Find people you respect and trust enough to tell you the truth. Open up to them and listen to their advice. You may not be able to save your current job, but you can prevent future derailment and lead a healthier life.

14. Derailment by Fantasy

"I am not a crook."—Richard Nixon

The popular image of business organizations is that they are places where logic and rationality reign supreme; where the bottom line and balance sheet override wishful thinking, false expectations and delusional thinking. That perception ultimately holds true. In order to survive over the long term, organizations need to bring in at least as much as they spend or they will expire. However, despite the objective, rationally derived, common denominator of the bottom line, business organizations are far from sterile illusion free institutions. Fantasies and delusions exist for both individuals and groups and, if not checked by reality, can result in derailment for either.

Hazard 59: Unrealistic Anticipation of Magical Change

If You Keep Hoping, Profits Will Come: The Hockey Stick Fantasy

Neil was an electrical engineer whose first job was with a startup computer company. They couldn't afford to pay him much but he received several generous stock options over his twelve years of employment. When he quit and sold his stock to start his own business, he had a substantial pot of money, most of which he managed to squander over a three year period by perpetuating the fantasy that his business would suddenly prosper.

Neil was conditioned by the early, freewheeling days of the mainframe computer and software development business where planning and organization took a backseat to innovation, enthusiasm and optimism. The orders just kept coming in, and despite the lack of valid forecasts, everyone had faith that they would continue. Technology was growing exponentially and the company operated under the planning equivalent of "if you build it, they will come."

Neil carried this business model, which by then was in rapid decline, into his new business. He hired far too many people, entered into a long-term lease for an inappropriately expensive facility and based his business on designing components and sub-assemblies for large mainframe computers. The market had shifted to much smaller business and personal computers and, aside from a few government orders, the business never took off. Revenues sagged and expenses soared; it was a going-out-of-business scenario but Neil was unable to come to grips with it.

At the beginning of every month he and his direct reports would hold a forecasting meeting. During these sessions his comptroller would present a series of graphs and charts, foremost of which was a graph showing time (month by month) on the horizontal axis and revenue on the vertical. Each month the graph would follow the classic hockey stick pattern; horizontally flat until the last few months, then rising sharply. The pattern migrated into annual forecasts. Each year, the chart would be recast with the flat handle of the hockey stick extending to the last months and, again, magically ascending.

Unlike some users of hockey stick forecasts, Neil had no data upon which to base the projected sharp increase in revenue. He just knew it would go up; he believed it and nothing could shake that belief. His fantasy was initially fueled by his past experience of unplanned bounty and, toward the end, by his inability to admit his dream had gone awry. He was a charismatic leader and many of his employees left his past employer to join him and shared the same cultural conditioning. As is characteristic of those who follow charismatic leaders, they had unshakable faith in his vision, didn't challenge his beliefs and shared his fantasy.

The group even acquired a humorous symbol of the recurring forecast. Neil's company was located in Minnesota where he grew up in a small town and played high school hockey. As time progressed, he developed the practice of bringing an old hockey stick to the forecast meetings and putting it on display on a table in front of his conference room. By the second quarter of the third year the humor turned to despair when it became clear that they were all colluding in a collective fantasy. There would be no magic source of revenue and Neil had run out of money to prop up the company. When he finally declared bankruptcy and closed the doors, Neil was angry, depressed and broke. Many of his employees shared his feelings but most had marketable skills and hadn't wasted their life's savings on a fantasy.

Driving Toward a Brick Wall with a Bottle and a Smile

Derailment by blind unsubstantiated faith that things aren't as bad as they seem and that a financial windfall awaits just over the horizon is certainly not the sole province of startups. A few years after Neil's departure, his former employer was in dire financial straits. It had exhausted its last line of credit, was experiencing a terminal cash flow problem, and the value of its stock had plummeted to a record low. A new executive with turnaround experience was hired. The second week after he arrived, he received an invitation to attend the firm's annual awards banquet where over a hundred employees experienced an open bar and dined on a gourmet feast. When asked to say a few words, he shocked the group. His fantasy-confronting statement was, "You remind me of a car full of people going ninety miles an hour toward a brick wall. Everyone is smiling and the driver is passing a bottle around."

The leaders of that firm were not alone in their happy road trip to destruction. The road to derailment is paved with organizational leaders who have been seduced by past success and are unable to comprehend the depth of their current problems. This can lead to the fantasy that things aren't as bad as they seem and that holding on and waiting for a brighter future to emerge is the best course of action. It usually takes an intervention—as in the board firing the top executive, an acquisition, or the addition of an empowered, action-oriented, outside executive—to burst the bubble of this self-destructive fantasy.

Hazard 60: The Ponzi Fantasy

The legacy of Italian con man Charles Ponzi, the Ponzi scheme pays existing investors from the contributions of new investors, not from the proceeds of actual investments. The scheme is doomed to eventually implode since it becomes impossible to secure a sufficient continuing supply of new money to pay the demands of existing investors. Prior to its inevitable collapse the scheme perpetrators collude in a shared fantasy that enough new money will keep coming and their confidence game won't be discovered.

The Ponzi scheme perpetrated by Bernard Madoff, that cost investors an estimated 50 billion dollars (Lenzer 2008), is considered the largest in U.S. history. It's unclear when Madoff actually started the scheme. Conservative estimates are that it lasted at least 20 years. During this time Madoff and his family were extremely financially and socially successful. He was even appointed chairman of the board of directors of the National Association of Securities Dealers. Deep down, at some level of consciousness, they must have known that they were living a lie and their house of cards was bound to collapse. But, they kept pushing forward, fueled by a collective fantasy that if they kept their heads in the sand, the good life would just continue to unfold. Reality shattered their fantasy when in 2008 Madoff was arrested; he is now serving a 150-year prison sentence. One son, Peter, has been sentenced to 10 years in prison and another, Mark, committed suicide two years after his father's arrest. It was a jolting derailment. The Madoff family paid a steep price for their collective fantasy.

A derivative of the Ponzi fantasy is the delusion held by some leaders that they can promise employees future pay raises and promotions and, even though they have no power or, at times, intention to deliver on those promises, things will work out in the end. The essence of that fantasy is the false belief that there will be no consequences for their unfulfilled promises. Research indicates that betrayal of trust is a primary reason for derailment (McCall and Lombardo 1983; Burke 2006). Leaders who don't deliver on their promises are not exempt. Richard's derailment is an example.

Hazard: 61: Making Undeliverable Promises

Blindsided and Unemployed in California: The Cost of Fantasy-Based Promises

Richard was the human resource manager of a manufacturing facility in Southern California. He reported to the plant manager, but had a functional reporting relationship to the vice president of human resources at his company's headquarters in a Minneapolis suburb. He started his career

14. Derailment by Fantasy

at the Minneapolis headquarters and was sent to California as a developmental assignment. He'd been there three years and wanted to return. A senior Minneapolis-based HR staff member was planning to retire in six months, and Richard was angling for her job.

Richard had a rocky tenure in California. He lacked grounding in the basic disciplines of HR—compensation administration, training and development, labor relations, and staffing—but was promoted based on his outgoing personality and ability to please others. Fortunately, he inherited a staff that was well qualified in these functions. Unfortunately, his need to be liked and his strategy of making commitments that he couldn't fulfill in order to please others got him in trouble. He operated under the fantasy that his promises were sufficient to build positive relationships and that there would be no lasting consequences if he failed to deliver.

The information technology manager lobbied the plant manager for approval to hire two additional people. Richard exhibited great empathy and promised the IT manager he'd convince the plant manager to approve the openings. The plant manager was struggling with a tight budget and didn't want to add any new employees. Richard knew that and, despite his promise, didn't advocate for the IT manager and the openings were not approved. The plant comptroller wanted an exception to the salary increase guidelines to reward and retain a key subordinate. Richard assured him the increase would be no problem. He knew that exceptions to salary increase guidelines needed to be approved by the compensation group in Minneapolis and also knew that the odds of that increase being approved were very slim. The amount was substantially reduced from what the manager recommended. There was an opening for a production supervisor and the department manager wanted to promote a marginally qualified white male. A very well qualified Hispanic woman in another department applied for the job. Richard wanted to make the manager happy more than he wanted to support the firm's affirmative action program and helped rig the system to promote the white male. The Hispanic woman filed a discrimination suit and the company settled with her rather than go to court. Richard's personal cost was a further erosion of his credibility.

Richard's career came to a halt when his labor relations expert quit. This staff member was very marketable, somewhat underpaid, and had an attractive external job offer. Richard promised a significant salary increase and a stock option if he would stay. He did deliver on the pay increase but had no authority to offer a stock option and it didn't happen. The labor relations expert quit during a critical time of union contract negotiations. Since Richard had no labor relations experience, his functional boss from Minnesota had to come to California and complete the negotiations. During the visit, she met with the division's managers and received a personal taste of the sour fruits of Richard's fantasy. During their final meeting, Richard was astonished. True to the blinders of his fantasy he thought there would be a promotion and a transfer back to Minneapolis. Instead he was offered a small severance package and a one way trip out the front door.

Hazard 62: Belief in a One-Dimensional Score Card

Senior military officers, experienced staff specialists, and externally funded non-profit leaders face a potentially derailing hazard when they move into line management positions in for-profit organizations. They have been conditioned to only deal with an expense budget and have no experience or appreciation for the criticality of the other side of the equation: the revenue budget. There are three ways this conditioning can lead to fantasy-oriented derailment.

The delusion of external assurance. The essence of this delusion is that, based on their past experience, another entity—a foundation, a government agency, a corporate staff function—has always had final responsibility for an adequate budget and has always delivered. The leader's job is simply to lobby for sufficient funds at budget time and live within dictated guidelines for the remainder of the year.

The delusion of a fixed, non-revenue dependent mission. This delusion is based on the false belief that the mission of leadership is to use externally derived funds to achieve plans and meet goals. The goals, plans, and funds are set in concrete during the budgeting period and are independent of the external market for the organization's goods or services.

The delusion of an internal focus. Leaders participating in this delusion believe that the essential task of the leader is to maintain and nurture an efficient and productive organization. Generating external revenue and adjusting the size and tactics of the organization to the vicissitudes of customer preferences is, at best, a distant, second-order priority.

I have found a surprising number of leaders who have succumbed to the fantasy of a one-dimensional score card. Some have derailed but the good news is that many have proven smart and flexible enough to eventually understand their prior conditioning did not transfer to the competitive, revenue-sensitive for-profit world.

Perspective and Advice

- Contrary to popular image, business organizations are not sterile and objective entities lead by the cold, clear quantitative dictates of a balance sheet. A closer examination will reveal dark corners where career-limiting fantasies and delusions lurk. The wise leader needs to avoid their traps. They have the potential to derail both individuals and organizations.
- Leaders whose values and mental models have been shaped and conditioned by outdated organizational cultures and economic trends are particularly susceptible to the fantasy that what worked in the past is still valid and will work in the future. Sagacious leaders have learned to continually seek external validation of their operating processes and mental models. Difficult though they may find it to discard comforting but invalid fantasies, they find the courage to let them go and embrace reality. If you are a leader and suspect your judgment and perceptions may be driven by the false assurance of a soothing fantasy, have the fortitude to seek external advice and feedback. If you don't and there is any validity to your suspicions, you and your employees may soon pass the point of no return on the road to derailment by fantasy.
- If you work for a boss whose response to a continual stream of valid data that reflects bad news is that "things aren't as bad as they seem," and whose strategic response is to "wait it out until things get back to normal," chances are you work for a person suffering from a stuck-in-the-past fantasy. You have three choices. You can try to change her by helping her drop the fantasy; you can keep your head down and wait for her to derail; or you can find a way out of the organization. The first two are risky; it's very difficult for a subordinate to make a boss confront a fantasy and, if you wait it out too long, she may take you with her when she derails. The best choice is to get out while you still can. The most optimistic option

would be to finagle an internal transfer. If that won't work leaving the organization is preferable to the pain of remaining and by doing so, perpetuating a career-limiting fantasy for both you and your boss.

- A very bad strategy is to engage in a dishonest or ethically sketchy practice, keep your head in the sand, reap the rewards, and collude by convincing yourself and others that it's really okay and will continue undetected into the future. It won't continue. The fantasy bubble will burst; reality will set in; you will be detected; and your career will be derailed.
- The fantasy of attempting to buy loyalty and respect by making promises you can't or don't want to keep and expecting that there will be no consequences is a lose/lose proposition. You will definitely lose the very respect you were trying to procure and there is a strong probability you will also lose your job.
- If you are moving into a for-profit business leadership role from a non-profit, staff, or military role, beware of the fantasy of only worrying about the expense side of the equation. You will need to adjust your orientation and alter your prior conditioning to focus on the generation of external revenue. You will need to be much more flexible in your structure and tactics to accommodate the whims of customers and changes in economic realities.

15. Derailment by Cross-Cultural Blindness

"Our global village has many disparate quarters."
—Geert Hofstede

While on the campaign trail in 1968, Maryland Governor Spiro Agnew put his future vice-presidential foot in his mouth when he called a reporter a "fat Jap." Although, in the overall context of his political career, it was a minor issue and didn't result in his derailment—revelations of bribes and corruption did that in 1973—it was indicative of the lack of cultural sensitivity that has caused many a promising career to go off track. The case study describing Phillip's derailment is a prime example.

Hazard 63: Cross-Cultural Managerial Incompetence

A Case Study: The Cost of Cultural Insensitivity

I came across Phillip while living in Australia. He was an American expatriate assigned to manage the Asian operations of a U.S.-headquartered electronics firm. He was on the fast track for a top leadership position and his appointment to the firm's Asian headquarters—which was actually located in Sydney—was a developmental assignment, meant to give him international experience. He was an electrical engineer who had risen up through the sales and marketing ranks. Prior to relocating to Australia, he had never lived away from Texas or traveled outside the United States. He was an extraverted technician with no real interest in cultural differences, world affairs, economic theories, or historical precedents.

His firm had an operation in Thailand and I was a firsthand observer of troubles to come when I accompanied him on his first visit, one month into his new job. During his initial meeting with the staff, he sat behind a table and put his cowboy boot-clad feet on top with the soles facing his employees. That's not even polite in Texas, but in the Thai culture it's a very serious insult. After being made aware of the issue, he compounded the problem during the second meeting when he put only one boot on the table and said, "I understand you people have some kind of a problem with my boots, so to prove I'm not a half bad guy, I'm only putting one up this time."

His attempt at humor may have passed muster in Houston, but in Bangkok it was greeted with silence and averted eyes. The Thai staff was both embarrassed by his cultural boorishness and angered by being labeled as "you people."

The third morning, he asked a secretary in front of her peers and her boss, the office manager, to meet with him, take shorthand, and type a report of his observations and recommendations. At the time of his visit, despite advances in technology, dictation and shorthand were commonly used in that office. She dutifully sat across from him and scribbled on a pad of paper while he dictated his report. He wanted it by the end of the day and the tension in the office rose in direct proportion to the proximity of quitting time.

At the end of the day, with bowed head and lowered eyes, she presented him with a barely legible page of gibberish. When it was explained to him that "face-saving" was an extremely powerful social norm in that culture and that she was neither skilled in shorthand, nor in English, and had simply faked it in order to save face, he again reacted the wrong way. Instead of finding a way to help in her face-saving by just accepting the report or indicating that he had changed his mind and didn't need it after all, he blew up and publicly berated the office manager. This accomplished two things: it caused the office manager to also lose-face, and violated another cultural norm by eroding the authority of the office manager's boss, the country director who, in a high power-distance culture like Thailand, should have been the one to privately chastise the office manager.

On the long flight back to Sydney, rather than admit he had misread the culture and had caused significant damage to his leadership credibility, he railed against their "oversensitivity," and angrily fumed that it was their obligation to understand him, as their boss, not the other way around. He didn't know it, but he was rapidly transiting the road to derailment based on his lack of cross-cultural competence.

Phillip was recalled nine months into his planned three-year assignment. Among the contributing factors was a disastrous individual incentive and recognition plan for his Japanese operation that ignored that country's highly collective culture. Its failure was highly visible to the U.S.–based top management team. He also managed to alienate his Australian staff, which was not easy given the tolerant Australian culture. They grew weary of his mocking, what he perceived as their "funny" accents, "strange" phraseology, and his putdowns concerning their small population and market size. His use of sarcasm-based humor was seen as cloddishness and cultural ignorance and not, as he presumed, cleverness.

The final blow came when he and his U.S.–based boss had dinner with a high level Australian government official and a few of his staff. The government was an important customer and the dinner was a feeling-out session for a future contract. In many countries, "educated" executives are expected to have a working knowledge of world affairs and global economics and the government representative, a rather pompous and formal bureaucrat, steered the conversation toward these two topics. After a few minutes and a few drinks, it became clear to his boss that Phillip hadn't a clue about either topic and his comments only revealed his lack of historical and economic literacy. Two weeks later he was on a plane back to Texas where his first appointment was with an outplacement firm.

Phillip's derailment was by no means unique. Studies vary in their criteria, approaches and conclusions, but it has been estimated that between 20 to 50 percent of expatriate assignments fail (Chalre' Associates 2014). Research shows that better selection, training, and orientation can reduce the odds (Tang 1987), but derailment by cross-cultural incompetence remains a significant problem and not just for expatriates residing outside of their home country. Employees with significant non–home country managerial responsibilities are also vulnerable.

Hazard 64: Not Understanding the Leadership Implications of Cross-Cultural Research

Hofstede's Pioneering IBM Study

Competent cross-cultural management begins with a basic understanding of the significant impact country and regional culture has on the way employees conceptualize work, leadership, and social interactions. In a pioneering study, Dutch researcher Geert Hofstede (1980) examined cultural differences among IBM's international population. He found that employees were as much, if not more, influenced by their country's culture than that of IBM. Among other findings he discovered significant differences in individual versus group identity and motivation, differences in comfort and acceptance of power and hierarchy, and differences in tolerance for ambiguity and the need for structure. In another early study, anthropologist Edward Hall (1976) divided country cultures into those where task and closure (low context cultures) were most valued and those where process and social interaction (high context cultures) were central. In my own early work (Noer 1975) awareness of cross-cultural differences was found to be key to management success and expatriate retention.

Although more recent studies have cast some doubt on Hofstede's methodology, his and Hall's pioneering studies have generally held true and have provided a foundation for a wide variety of cross-cultural leadership research, all of which substantiate substantial differences in cultural values and their implications for effective leadership. In my later research (Noer 2006, 2007, 2008), I have found significant differences between American, Saudi Arabian, French, German, English, and Indian managerial coaching, learning tactics and leadership behaviors.

It's not necessary for cross-cultural leaders to have an in-depth understanding of all the research, but it is essential that they have a grasp of basic concepts such as high and low context cultures, cultural differences in the use and acceptance of power, and variations in individual versus group identity and motivation. Without understanding and applying these differences to their leadership styles, they will be flying blind and, as was illustrated in Phillip's case study, be susceptible to derailment based on that blindness.

Cross-Cultural Blindness in Action: Five Examples

These examples of cross-cultural blind spots may not individually cause derailment, but when repeated and linked, they form a behavioral pattern that certainly has that potential. They are presented here from a Western, primarily American, orientation. Cultures with different values and norms will find them useful to better understand and react to incidents of U.S.-oriented cross-cultural blindness. They are outlined as hazards 65–70.

Hazard 65: *Prematurely Pressing for Closure*

In low context cultures task trumps process. Getting the job done, reaching closure, not getting distracted by personal issues and sticking to business are the operant values. Most Anglo cultures are classified as low context and the U.S. is among the lowest of the low. Here is a paraphrased, abbreviated version of a scene that demonstrates what happens when a low context manager is blind to the process values of a high context customer.

The U.S. manager has flown from his firm's headquarters in Milwaukee to Mexico City, checked into his hotel, quickly freshened up, and has taken a cab to his customer's office where he hopes to conclude a lengthy long distance—phone and internet—negotiation involving the sale of heavy construction equipment. His objective is to get the contract signed and catch the first flight back. This is the first time he has met the customer face-to-face.

After a brief round of introductory small talk, the U.S. manager opens his briefcase and pulls out a sheaf of contractual documents. "How was your trip?" asks the customer, making eye contact and ignoring the contracts.

"Fine, everything was on time," responds the manager, pushing the contracts across the desk toward the customer.

"And how is your family?" asks the customer, moving his gaze to the photograph of his own wife and children on his desk.

"They're good," the manager abruptly responds, ignoring the cue and holding out the contracts. "I think we covered all the details during our last phone conference. If you don't have any questions, we can get on with it. I have copies for you and we can find a couple of witnesses, get them signed and affix your company seal or whatever legal paraphernalia you people use down here."

The customer, irritated by what he views as the impolite pushiness of the manager and insulted by the put-down term "you people," calls upon his reserve of patience and tries again.

"What are your plans for dinner?" he asks.

The manager, again missing the cue, responds, "Well, after we get these contracts signed, I plan on going back to my hotel room, catching up on some paperwork, having a quick bite through room service, getting some rest, and catching the morning flight back."

And so it went. The customer, driven by the social norms of his high context culture wanted to establish a personal relationship before committing to a business relationship. The manager, a cross-culturally blind product of a low context culture left the session frustrated by the customer's reluctance to get down to business and his focus on personal issues.

The manager returned to Milwaukee with unsigned contracts and his firm nearly lost the order. A more seasoned, internationally experienced executive returned to Mexico, spent the requisite time and established the necessary personal relationship and the transaction eventually materialized.

Hazard 66: Misreading Appropriate Social Distance

Hall (1966) used the term "proxemics" to describe differing cultural standards of acceptable social space. Comfortable social distance varies by culture. The U.S., Norway, and Germany, represent "cool" cultures where comfortable business interactions require more distance. Vietnam, China and Japan are representative of countries that prefer closer distances for business interactions and Brazil, Mexico and Italy have "warm" cultures with a preference for even closer interaction distances.

Observation and the ability to step out of one's comfort zone is an important cross-cultural skill. When people from warm cultures interact with business associates from cool cultures they often cause discomfort by violating comfort zones reserved only for personal friends. If they move even closer, they cross the boundaries reserved for intimate interactions and can cause extreme distress. Careful observers at meetings may be treated to a classic "proxemic dance," typified by an Italian having a conversation with a Norwegian. The closer the Italian gets, the more he violates the social space of the Norwegian and the more the Norwegian moves away. The more the Norwegian moves away, the more the Italian moves in. They are partners in a proxemic dance to the music of cross-cultural blindness.

15. Derailment by Cross-Cultural Blindness

On a trip to Saudi Arabia a few years ago, I observed the effect of both proxemic and haptic (non-verbal communication involving touch) cross-cultural blindness. My client was a very senior petroleum executive. I'd worked with him often in the past and we were friends as well as business associates. After a very long, exhausting flight, I and an associate who had never been to Saudi Arabia before were rushed to a welcoming dinner. I was seated next to my executive friend and he immediately entered what, to my Western conditioning would be my intimate space, conversing just a few inches from my face. He expressed his sympathy for my jet lag by making eye contact and putting his hand on my leg.

When we returned to the hotel, my colleague expressed amazement that "an out-of-the-closet, gay, top executive" would behave in such a provocative manner with a guest in the presence of his staff. I explained that I had no idea what the executive's sexual orientation was, but his meeting behavior was solely the result of cultural values, nothing else. When with friends, male Saudis often kiss each other, hold hands, converse at a close proxemic distance, and, when making a point or expressing empathy, touch the other person.

Research has shown that non-verbal behavior is much more important to the impressions we make than the words we say. Cross-cultural blindness around differences in the use of personal space or comfort with touching, can, at best, result in misunderstanding and discomfort. At worse it can result in alienating clients and losing customers.

Hazard 67: Insensitivity to Power-Distance Values

Power-distance defines the cultural acceptance and accommodation of inequality. High power-distance cultures are comfortable with authoritarian leadership and sharp differences in status and pay. Disagreeing with, or causing the leader to lose face is counter to the norm. Low power-distance cultures are the opposite. Israel and the Scandinavian countries are among the top low-power distance countries. Malaysia, the Philippines, and the Arab countries are among the top high-power distance countries.

An example of the effect of cross-cultural blindness to power-distance values took place in a team-building session. The facilitators were from

Australia—a low power-distance country and the participants were Saudis—Saudi Arabia is a country with a high power-distance culture. The initial Saudi group was made up of a manager and his direct reports. Although not part of the plan, the manager's boss also decided to attend. Consistent with high power-distance norms, the manager didn't tell his boss it was a bad idea for him to attend. In accordance with their cross-cultural blindness, the facilitators let it happen, even though they knew that two levels of management were hard to work with. They'd done it in before in Australia and thought they could handle it in Jeddah.

Jeddah wasn't Sydney. The session was a disaster. Many of the team's problems were a result of the style and decisions of the bosses' boss. Striving for authenticity and conditioned by low power-distance tolerance for criticizing the boss, they facilitated an exercise that gave him open, public feedback. He became defensive, accusatory, and angrily walked out of the session. The participants were embarrassed and accused the facilitators of betraying confidential information. The team's leader canceled the session and the Australians returned to Sydney, losing a customer but gaining insight into cross-cultural differences.

Hazard 68: Imposing Individualistic Systems on Collectivist Cultures

The example of Phillip's failed attempt to install an incentive plan based on his U.S. (individualistic) culture in a Japanese (collectivist culture) organization is an illustration of cross-cultural blindness in action. The collectivist orientation extends beyond the business world as anyone who has encountered the ubiquitous groups of Japanese enjoying vacations together knows. Contrast that experience with the very rare Norwegian or Danish (both highly individualistic cultures) practice of large group vacations.

Whether it be implementing a policy, negotiating a joint venture, or selling a product, representatives of individually oriented cultures need to exhibit patience, tolerance for consensus building, and accommodation of multiple interests when dealing with the many collectivist cultures in the world. Insensitivity to collectivist values and attempting to force fit individualistic approaches are evidence of cross-cultural blindness and usually doomed to failure.

Hazard 69: Rigid Adherence to a Sequential Time Orientation

There are two very different culturally defined concepts of time (Trompennars 1993). Sequential time is the U.S. norm. "Time is money" is the defining label. Appointments are kept, schedules are adhered to, relationships are subordinate to schedules, and plans, once developed, are destined to be followed.

Synchronic time is the norm in many Latin American, and a number of other, cultures. "Mañana is good enough for me" is the inaccurate label used by cross-culturally blind managers with sequential time conditioning. In synchronic time cultures, tasks are done concurrently and one is not necessarily finished before another is initiated. Appointments and schedules are approximate, variable, and flexible. Relationships usually trump schedules. Time is a relative, not an absolute, concept.

On the second, deal-saving Mexican visit by an experienced non-cross-culturally blind executive from the Milwaukee heavy equipment firm, negotiations were secondary to relationships, there was no set time schedule or established agenda. Synchronic time guided the process and the executive flew back to Wisconsin with a done deal.

Contrary to U.S. cultural conditioning sequential time is not better than the synchronic variety. Both are artifacts of cultural values. The non-cross-culturally blind leader, when working with the opposite cultural preference, will step back, take a deep breath, and adjust his approach from sequential to synchronic time in order to be effective.

Perspective and Advice

- Cross-cultural management requires both an understanding of the different ways country and regional cultures shape employee values and motivation and the ability to adjust your leadership style to these differences. Anything else will put you on a slippery slope to derailment whether you are an in-country expatriate or operate from your home country.
- The U.S. is an individualistic, low context culture and many of the growing economies outside the U.S. are much more group oriented and blend social and business interactions. Without understanding

and adapting to these differences, managers will not serve their careers or their organizations well.
- Expatriate selection and training are the keys to success. Too many firms select the best technical person for management. The results are that they, often, lose a good technician and gain a bad manager. In terms of the consequences, the mistake is significantly amplified when applied to selecting someone to work in another culture. Even with positive home country managerial results, there is no guarantee that home country managerial skills and values will carry over to a foreign assignment. An understanding of cultural differences, a high tolerance for ambiguity, self-understanding and a basic grounding in economics and history are requisite skills.
- If you are tapped for an expatriate assignment or a significant international management role, think long and hard before accepting. If you work and live in another culture you will be tested in many more ways than had you remained in your home country. The expatriate failure rate is high and you need to view your assignment as an adventure that requires learning, not a sentence that equates to punching a promotional ticket. If you have a family, a move to a different culture can either be a positive bonding and learning experience or a path to friction, separation and career derailment.

PART VI
MISDIRECTED LOYALTIES

The chapters in this section provide strategies to escape the hazards of misdirected loyalties. Unyielding loyalty to an organizational sub-unit, commitment to a non-diverse team, or over-reliance on a single discipline can lead to derailment. As one ascends perches in the totem pole or changes organizational affiliation, the functional fixedness hazard lurks for those with one-dimensional adherence to a functional specialty or a single business model. The diversity adversity hazard awaits those who develop lock step teams. Those who motivate and bond subordinates around disparagement of other units and individuals are scripting a formula for both individual and organizational derailment.

Part VI Chapter Summary

The Three Categories of Incompatible Needs Risk and How to Navigate Them

Derailment Risks	*What to Do About Them*
Chapter 16: Functional Fixedness: Applying your functional skills and strategic orientation to a problem that requires a different perspective.	Have the courage to move out of your functional comfort zone and more objectively diagnose and respond to problems and strategic choices.
Chapter 17: Diversity Adversity: creating narrow, non-diverse work groups and teams.	Resist the temptation to build a team of people who think, look, and act like you. The most powerful and creative teams are differentiated by their diversity.
Chapter 18: Sub-Unit Arrogance: Building a team around hostility, superiority and sarcasm directed at other organizational units or individuals.	Establish and reinforce a norm of accommodating and supporting other organizational units. Know that building a team based on a foundation of arrogance is fragile, self-serving, and it will ultimately crumble.

16. Derailment by Functional Fixedness

> "We shape our tools and thereafter our tools shape us."—*Marshall McLuhan*

Functional fixedness is one of those strange alliterative phrases that can sometimes be found in the behavioral sciences. This one has roots in the Gestalt branch of psychology and, unusual though it may sound, has serious implications for career longevity. In psychological terms, it involves getting stuck in a one-dimensional mental model. In business terms, it means over-reliance on a single functional skill set or a previously successful strategic option.

Using the Box to Think Outside the Box

In a classic experiment that illustrates the concept of functional fixedness (Adamson 1952), participants were given a candle, a book of matches and a box of thumb tacks. Their task was to attach the candle to the wall so that it didn't drip wax onto the table below. Most participants tried to melt the candle and attach it to the wall or pin it with the tacks. Very few considered melting the candle so that it stuck to the bottom of the box and then tacking the box to the wall. Their "fixedness" involved being stuck on perceiving that the only function of the box was to hold the tacks. The participants were unable to "think outside the box" and use the box in a unique way. Derailment by functional fixedness occurs because people are stuck inside a functional or strategic box and are unable to escape it and use more relevant approaches.

There are three dimensions of functional fixedness that can lead to career derailment. The first is discipline-conditioned. It involves being stuck within the paradigmatic boundaries of one business function with the inability to view issues through other functional lenses. The second entails fixation with one only strategic orientation. The third is being stuck in a management style that no longer fits the current reality.

Hazard 70: Functional Blinders

Discipline-conditioned functional fixedness tends to appear hierarchically; the higher one rises, the stronger the hazard. Some people have a great deal of difficulty dropping their functional orientation when promoted to general management roles. The senior executive coming out of the financial function can fall into the trap of applying financial lenses to all problems and potential solutions. It happens in all disciplines and, as illustrated in the case of Bernie the psychologist, the hazards of discipline-conditioned functional fixedness are a narrow perspective, misdiagnosis of root problems, and application of an inappropriate strategy.

Bernie's Derailment: The Cost of Functional Blinders

A colleague and I tried to help Bernie, an industrial and organizational psychologist who was hired to lead a management consulting firm. We'd worked with him in the past and were flattered that he asked for our help. We soon discovered that, even with his professional background and experience, he was trapped in his functional blinders. In fact, they were attached with the psychological equivalent of unbreakable Gorilla Glue.

His presenting problem was that, regardless of his long hours, seemingly innovative approach and tenacious persistence, the numbers kept eroding; expenses were up, revenue was down, morale was waning, and the firm was losing long-term clients. His view from inside his blinders was that he needed to improve things by developing a participative management system and building cross-functional teams. He spent a lot of time—and time was truly money in his type of consulting business—conducting off-site sessions and attempting to facilitate employee buy-in for these initiatives.

Our conclusions were that, although these were all worthy initiatives, the real problems were obsolete products, too many non-revenue producing employees, and the lack of a viable marketing plan. He carefully listened to our recommendations and went through the motions of asking the right questions but we could tell he got it in his head, but not in his heart or his feet.

Bernie was stuck within his functional blinders and couldn't escape. He halfheartedly implemented one of our suggestions and ignored the rest. Two weeks after we left, he asked us to facilitate a team-building workshop in advance of a group session he planned to better articulate the firm's mission, vision, and core values. It was clear to us that he was driving his functional car above the speed limit the wrong way on a one-way street with the gage on empty and no gas stations in sight. We cut our fee in half, declined further involvement and, sadly, waited for the predictable ending.

Three months later it happened. The firm folded, some of their products and a small number of employees were picked up by a competitor and our former colleague contacted us again, this time seeking a job. We, again, declined but did make some progress in helping him understand the steep price he paid for those stubborn functional blinders.

Hazard 71: Strategic Blinders

CEOs are not immune to derailment by functional fixedness and it is usually of the strategic or style variety. It most often occurs when they are hired from outside a corporation to "fix" problems. As in the story of the old western gunfighter who was made sheriff to clean up the town but the town remained dirty and the sheriff became the problem, externally recruited CEOs sometimes discover that the guns they toted in previous roles don't work in their new environment. After a few costly misfires and shooting some strategic blanks, they are shown the door. At one level it's difficult to feel sorry for them because when they inevitably are fired by their boards, they depart with large severance packages. On the other hand, they have failed, been involuntary terminated, and even if they appear to land on their feet, their egos and reputations have paid a steep price.

JCPenney Isn't Apple: Ron Johnson's Derailment

Ron Johnson's failure as JCPenney's CEO is an example of derailment by fixation on a strategy that didn't fit the corporation's environment. Prior to JC Penney he was the senior vice president of retail operations at Apple and was the architect of Apple's highly successful, trendy, hip, gadget-filled retail stores. Upon joining JC Penney in November of 2011, he immediately, with no market testing, attempted to transform shopping at JC Penney into a chic, boutique-like destination experience featuring stores with no coupons or sales. He misread customer preferences, the shopping environment desired by core customers, and the attraction of the JC Penney brand (Tuttle 2013). His fixation on attempting to force the Apple strategy into the Penney culture derailed him. He was fired in April of 2013.

Hewlett-Packard Isn't SAP: Leo Apotheker's Derailment

The very short-term (11 month) tenure of Leo Apotheker as CEO of Hewlett-Packard was another very expensive, in terms of both severance pay ($25 million) and in company performance (40 percent decline in stock price), example of derailment by strategic fixedness. Apotheker headed the large software firm SAP prior to joining Hewlett-Packard in November of 2010. Hewlett-Packard was primarily a hardware company with software making up only two percent of the firm's revenue. However, true to the dictates of strategic functional fixation, Apotheker attempted to refocus the business on high margin products such as cloud computing and software (Goldman 2011). Although Hewlett-Packard's board has never been accused of strategic consistency or thoughtful hiring—firing three successive CEOs in the five years prior to Apotheker—an understanding of the hazards of the strategic variety of functional fixation might have prevented another mistake.

Hazard 72: Style Blinders

The Derailment of Andrew Mason

Fixation with a style of leadership that may have worked in the past but does not fit the current environment or the future vision is a blueprint for derailment. It often occurs when an entrepreneur is unable to let go of the style and organizational culture that helped in the start-up phase but blocks the more structured and administratively oriented culture necessary for sustained performance. Andrew Mason, the founder and CEO of Groupon, honestly stated the outcome of his fixation with an unstructured, make it up as you go along, start-up culture, in his letter to employees the day he was fired, February 28, 2013 (Paczkowski 2013 1):

> After four and a half intense and wonderful years as CEO of Groupon, I've decided that I'd like to spend more time with my family. Just kidding—I was fired today. If you're wondering why, you haven't been paying attention. From controversial metrics in our S1 to our material weakness to two quarters of missing our own expectations and a stock price that's hovering around one quarter of our listing price, the events of the last year and a half speak for themselves. As CEO, I am accountable.

Relieving Groupon of a culture nurtured by the style functional fixedness of its founder had immediate positive effects on the organization. Eric Lefkofsky, the new CEO reported that "Morale is dramatically better than it was under Andrew Mason" (Carlson 2013 1). Four months after his departure, Groupon's stock more than doubled from its price when he was terminated.

Hazard 73: Retreating to a Past Comfort Zone

Stress can trigger regression into a previous functional comfort zone. This phenomenon can be seen at any minor league baseball park. Most young pitchers get to the minors because of their fast ball. Part of their development is learning to throw and control a curve. In a tight situation when the game is on the line, even though a breaking ball is the right call, they will, to the frustration of their coaches, stubbornly advocate and occasionally unilaterally revert to a fast ball. Another example can be found on the golf course. Most amateur golfers are plagued by a tendency to slice the ball, causing it to bend off target to the right. I have a friend who spent a lot of money on lessons and learned to overcome his slice and even, when called for, could hit a controlled hook—moving the ball from right to left. However, in stressful situations such as when a match or a wager is at stake, he regresses to his previous comfort zone and aims well to the left, hoping his slice will bring the ball back in play. This sometimes works but slices are difficult to control and there are trees and water hazards that make his reversion to this previous comfort zone costly to him and profitable to his opponents.

Sam's Demotion: A Study of Regression in Action

Stress-induced regression to a previous functional comfort zone happens frequently in business organizations and, if it becomes a recurring

16. Derailment by Functional Fixedness

pattern, can lead to derailment. One example occurred with Sam, a very successful sales manager who was promoted to a general management position. Initially his business environment was relatively stable and he was able to move away from his functional conditioning, adopt a balanced approach, and access the perspectives of other functions. The vice president, to whom Sam reported, gave him a large salary increase and a glowing performance evaluation nine months after his promotion.

Not long after, the situation changed. His firm, an electronic components manufacturer, lost a large customer that was a stable source of revenue. A new Asian competitor bought their way into the market by significantly lower pricing and, to further complicate matters, the patent protection for their most profitable product was about to expire. The former sales manager was faced with a set of strategic, financial, and product development issues but, rather than address them, he reverted back to his functional conditioning. He tried to sell his way out of the problem.

At a time when expenses needed to be cut and the workforce reduced, Sam hired additional salespeople. Rather than develop new products and services that provided a market differentiation and competitive advantage, he created incentive plans that were designed to spur the sales force to flog the same old, overpriced, non-competitive products that were in vogue when he was the sales manager. Sam's boss saved his bacon by forming a task force, chairing it himself, and facilitating a series of actions that put the operation back on track. Sam managed to keep his job but his second performance appraisal was far from glowing and there was no salary increase.

In the year that followed Sam seemed to rise above his functional fixation and adopt a balanced approach. Once again, however, he reverted back to his comfort zone when things got rough. This time the triggering event was an acquisition. His division was sold to a competitor—that pesky Asian firm. Decisions were being made on who would lead the new organization and Sam was the prime candidate. His demise was a presentation to the board of the acquiring firm.

The Asians wanted Sam's division for its products, patents, and development staff, not for its sales force. If he had taken the time to analyze the situation and access the perspectives of other functions, Sam would have kept his general management position. Instead, he orchestrated a PowerPoint–aided pep rally, touting the attributes of his sales force and recommending a new structure with more salespeople and an additional level of management.

Sam was demoted to his past role as sales manager, his salary was cut, the new structure was not approved, and a new general manager was hired through a search firm. He was a victim of serial regression to an inappropriate functional comfort zone. The difficulty with Sam's form of functional fixedness is that it is masked and only appears during times of stress. Permanently moving from a pattern of functional regression is an against-the-grain experience requiring self-awareness and motivation by the individual and coaching and patience by the boss.

Perspective and Advice

- Functional fixedness is a strange term but it has a profound impact on career longevity. There is a strong probability that a fixation on a single functional discipline such as IT or accounting will result in derailment when one moves up the organizational hierarchy into a general management role. A fixation with one leadership style or organizational culture also has a high probability of triggering derailment when the organization moves through successive stages of growth and maturation. The threat of derailment by cultural functional fixedness is significantly increased when an organization moves out of a start-up phase or is acquired by a firm with a different culture.
- The way to avoid derailment by functional fixedness is to become proficient in the process of holding on and letting go. There are some things—behaviors, cultural orientations, roles played—that fit past environments, but if carried into the future get in the way. There are other things—core values and basic beliefs—that irrespective of the time and place, need to remain. Almost all derailments by functional fixedness result from not letting go of the former.
- Visualize a series of gymnastic rings hanging by ropes. A person jumps from a platform and grabs a ring with the right hand, then—while maintaining momentum—reaches out and grabs the next ring with the left hand; then, again, grasps the next ring with the right, keeping the rhythm and moving through a line of successive rings. If that person is you, you have to let go of one ring before you can grab hold of another, and there comes a moment of truth when, if

16. Derailment by Functional Fixedness

you want to continue to move, you have neither hand on a ring but must have faith that you will have the ability to grasp the ring in front of you. If you don't let go, you will lose momentum and will be stuck, unable to grasp the next ring. You'll be hanging in mid-air and, although you may be able to keep your grip for a while, you will eventually weaken and drop to the ground. As you look up and see others traversing the rings, you become aware that for wont of the courage to let go, you have been derailed by functional fixedness.

- Stress-induced regression to a comfortable, though no longer appropriate, function, strategy or style is a pervasive hazard. Wise leaders seek feedback on the relevance of all three. Wise and successful leaders "hear" the feedback and have the courage to resist the false assurance of fixedness that no longer fits.
- Overcoming functional fixedness requires both the courage to let go and the ability look in the mirror and face what you see. It almost always requires at least one other pair of eyes to help you focus. If you are considering a role that takes you out of your functional comfort zone make sure you really understand the degree of your inclination toward functional fixedness. If the compass is too hard wired, you either need to stay in your current comfort zone or work very hard to muster up the courage and gain the skills that will allow you to let go.

17. Derailment by Diversity Adversity

"Strength lies in differences, not in similarities."
—*Stephen Covey*

In today's global, networked, highly competitive organizational environment, the days of the isolated individual contributor are gone. In order to make informed decisions and respond to rapidly changing technology, customer preferences, and diverse cultural values, working effectively in groups is a matter of survival. Most business schools and corporate management development programs spend far too little time and energy teaching future leaders the requisite skills and perspectives for leading and forming effective teams. Central to this learning is the criticality of diverse teams. The penalty for not creating them, as illustrated by the case of Jack, can be derailment.

Hazard 74: Creating a Team of Puppets

The Demise of a Puppeteer

I and a colleague interviewed all of Jack's direct reports as a prelude to a team development process. We were puzzled by the results. Most members of an organizational unit have a wealth of diverse and sometimes conflicting ideas and suggestions concerning team performance and priorities. The acceptance and open airing of ideological diversity is essential to effective team performance and can lead to innovation, goal clarity, and increased productivity.

In the case of Jack's group—we called them a group because they never achieved the synergy required to be classified as a team—all but one person denied any conflict, supported all of Jack's past decisions, and saw no need

17. Derailment by Diversity Adversity   145

to examine the groups operating process. They were suspiciously uniform in resisting any suggestions that the group or Jack could be more effective by making some changes. The only outlier was the newest member, a young African American woman hired directly after graduating from college and put in her new job as a part of the firm's affirmative action program. Not only were her perceptions of the group's effectiveness unique, she differed physically; the other group members, as was Jack, were middle-age white males.

Studies have shown that effective teams are not only comfortable and energized by openly airing differences, but also that members assume unique complimentary roles in order to facilitate team effectiveness (Benne and Sheats 1948; Belbin 2010). There are two types of group roles in productive teams: maintenance and task. Maintenance roles are those that help a team resolve conflict, and ensure balanced participation. Labels for members performing these roles are "harmonizers" and "gatekeepers." Task roles help teams stay focused, accomplish objectives, and confront productivity blockages. These roles have names such as "implementer" and "shaper/challenger." My real world experience confirms the validity of this research. The most effective teams are comprised of members who have evolved into specialized task and maintenance roles. In the case of Jack's team, with the exception of the new college graduate, the members assumed only one uniform role: puppet.

Jack worked for a financial services firm and was in charge of a number of small, storefront consumer loan offices located throughout the southeastern United States. The operating mode of these offices was conservative, risk averse, and blindly compliant with corporate directives and procedures. Jack worked his way up from one of these offices as did, with the exception of the recently hired new gradate, all of his direct reports. They were all "lifers," having spent their entire careers with the firm and were planning to retire from it. Of Jack's ten subordinates, five attended the same college and all but four were members of the same Southern Baptist Church.

Jack, however, differed from his subordinates in one, very telling, respect. We administered the FIRO-B, an assessment instrument that measures, among other dimensions, the desire to control others compared to the comfort with being controlled by others (Schnell, 1993). He was at the top of the scale in his desire to control others and at the bottom on his comfort with being controlled. In contrast, most of his direct reports reported low to moderate needs to control others and relatively high comfort with being controlled. Not that the FIRO-B is a totally valid and reliable psychometric instrument, but it provided insight into the kind of people Jack selected to work for him and his own intolerance for dissention.

Jack's firm was acquired by a holding company with a much more flexible and entrepreneurial culture. He resisted their attempts to consolidate and grow his small offices and broaden their product offerings. His group, with the predictable exception of the outlier, colluded in his resistance. None were willing or able to accept a change or visualize a new environment with broader opportunities. This lack of group ideological and conceptual diversity contributed to Jack's derailment and that of several of his group members. Despite strong messages to be more open and flexible both in his management style and his organizational structure, he dug his heels in and his group followed suit. Dug-in heels were not compatible with the culture of the new owners. Jack was terminated, a short-term replacement helped create a more diverse and flexible team, and eighteen months later, the then not so new college graduate was put in charge.

Requisite Skills for Leading Diverse and Creative Teams

Early research at the Center for Creative Leadership pointed out that building a narrow team and hiring in the leader's own image were prime derailment factors (McCall and Lombardo 1983). Since then we have experienced rapidly accelerated achievements in technology, a globalized marketplace, and cross-cultural economic interdependence. Organizations today are operating in a much more complex environment and the need for diverse, open, and creative teams is even more important. Building and leading diverse teams is an essential survival skill for effective leadership. I have found that there are five keys to building creative teams, conducting authentic meetings, and minimizing the potential of individual or team derailment. These are outlined as hazards 75 through 80.

Hazard 75: Intolerance of Outliers

Team members who think differently, have unique skills, and have different cultural values should be encouraged, not shut down. Although Jack, in the previous example was a hard case, had he and his team of puppets

17. Derailment by Diversity Adversity

been open to the "different" new graduate's ideas and encouraged their expression they might have learned something and, albeit chances of this were somewhat slim, they might have had a chance to avoid derailment.

Hazard 76: Top-Down, One-Dimensional Leadership

The formal leader does not have a corner on knowledge, ideas, or group process. Technical experts should lead technical discussions and facilitate technical decisions. Those who hold different values, come from other cultures, or represent different generations should lead and help the group focus on their unique perspectives. The formal leader should take a back seat whenever possible and let the group share responsibility for effective meetings.

Hazard 77: Lack of Focus and Concern Over How the Group Operates

Far too many teams take neither the time, nor the risk, to examine their group dynamics. The most effective teams continually examine how they are working together, the balance between maintenance and task roles, and interpersonal relationships. Without consciously working on group process, team creativity and synergy will atrophy. It may require finding an external facilitator, but the results will be well worth the cost and time.

Hazard 78: Leaders Who Don't Solicit or Value Team Feedback

No team leader is perfect and all have blind spots. In today's diverse and competitive environment, no leader can afford to have too large a blind spot. Those who want to minimize the chances of individual and team derailment find ways to reduce their blind spots through feedback. The primary source is team members. The primary lubricants are trust and a mutual desire to increase team effectiveness.

Hazard 79: Joyless and Stressful Meetings

I have found the harbingers of both team and leader derailment are glum, depressing, heavy, humorless, meetings. When both the leader and the participants look pained and complain of the waste of attending "another damn useless meeting," it's a very bad sign. Effective, spontaneous, diverse and creative teams see meetings as an adventure, not a sentence. Tightly controlled, time-constrained, rigid agendas, overly formal, boss-dominated meetings are the enemy of creativity and the friend of derailment.

Hazard 80: Overlooking Style and Decision-Making Diversity When Creating Teams

The Insufficiency of Race, Gender and Age: A Case Study

Non-profit organizations are not immune to the productivity-inhibiting effects of lockstep, homogenous teams. It has been my experience that they often tend to be less diverse in their approach to gathering and analyzing data and making decisions than their counterparts in for-profit business organizations.

Some colleagues and I recently did some pro-bono work for a community-based non-profit organization that was focused on helping homeless people get off the street, find jobs, and rid themselves of disabling addictions. At first glance, it would be hard to find a more diverse organization. Their board was large and made up of a blend of African Americans, Hispanics, and Whites. There was a healthy mix of males and females and a variety of ages. They constituted an array of race, gender, and age but they were not differentiated by the type of diversity required for effective teamwork.

The requisite diversity extends beyond race, gender, and age. Effective teams need members who assess problems, solutions, and strategies differently and operate within a climate that allows them to articulate their perspectives, hear others, learn from each other, and develop creative outcomes.

A popular instrument used in team assessment and development is the Myers-Briggs Type Indicator (Briggs Myers 1998). It measures individual preferences in the way team members gather data and make decisions Like the FIRO-B, the Myers-Briggs is not totally valid and reliable, but it provides an excellent practical way to assess the degree of team diversity.

I have found, and most research supports my experience, that the most effective and creative teams are made up of members with a variety of Myers-Briggs data gathering and decision-making preferences.

We administered the Myers-Briggs to the entire board and discovered a remarkable similarity—lack of diversity—in the way they performed the two primary group functions of gathering data and making decisions. Almost all the members had a strong preference for using their internally generated intuition for gathering information. This, in contrast to the other data gathering method measured by the Myers-Briggs: direct sensing of information from the external environment. The second aspect of the board members' homogenous responses was in the way they made decisions. The instrument differentiates between people who make decisions based on analysis, "thinkers," and those who base their decisions on emotions, "feelers." Nearly all the members had a preference for basing their decisions on feeling.

The board gave us two related presenting problems. The first was a sharp reduction in funding—the city and county governments had their own budget issues and cut their contributions by half of the amount they gave the previous year. The second was a huge increase in need. The recession had put more people on the street and they desperately needed help. The fundamental issue was that the organization was a group of nice people wanting to help with a significant social problem but were hampered by their one-dimensional style. Hard decisions needed to be made based on hard data and these decisions needed to be made with hard heads, not soft hearts. Until they could secure other sources of funding, they needed to drastically reduce their services and only concentrate on meeting a fraction of the needs.

In Myers-Briggs terms, they needed many more thinkers and sensors to offset their bias for feeling and intuition. In contrast, many business organizations are non-diverse in the other direction. The predominant management preferences in business organizations are sensing and thinking. Effective teams—either non-profit or for-profit—require a diverse mix of data-gathering and decision-making styles.

Tricky Dick and Honest Abe: A Contrast in Creating Diverse Teams

For a vivid historical contrast in the value of team diversity one has only to compare the staffs of Presidents Richard Nixon and Abraham Lincoln.

Nixon and his two closest advisors, Domestic Advisor John Ehrlichman and Chief of Staff H.R. Haldeman shared similar California-based political roots. They constituted a closed, distrustful, plotting, paranoiac trio (Weiner 2015). Watergate derailed all three.

Goodwin (2005) captured the essence of President Lincoln's opposite approach in the title of her Pulitzer-winning book, *A Team of Rivals*. Lincoln appointed his presidential rivals to his cabinet, learned from them, and channeled their diversity and contrasting styles to enrich his administration.

Perspective and Advice

- Building a team around people who think like you, come from a similar background, and are either unable or unwilling to challenge your ideas is a road to team ineffectiveness and probable personal derailment.
- Closed, lockstep conformity may provide more comfort and easier management, but it won't help you or your team survive in today's complex and competitive environment.
- Creating a diverse team involves much more than dealing with issues of age, race and gender. It requires building a team with members who have diverse ways of conceptualizing problems and poising strategic options. It necessitates developing and nurturing team members who fulfill vital team maintenance and task roles. It requires members who have the ability to learn from each other and build on different perspectives.
- Leading a truly diverse team requires the courage to resist over controlling, the patience to allow productive dialogue to occur, and the faith that group decisions are, in most cases, much better than individual dictates. Difficult though it may be, if you don't pursue team leadership with these attributes, your team will not contribute to the organizational goals and you will increase the odds of your individual derailment.
- If you find yourself a member of a non-diverse, closed, top-down, lockstep team, you have the basic fight or flight response options. In my experience, attempting to change the style of a locked-in, ineffective leader is almost always a dead end proposition so the

"fight" response usually involves waiting her out. The predictable derailment sometimes takes a long time to materialize and the hazard of waiting it out is that you can be stereotyped as "one of her people," and you may also go down with her sinking ship. Unless you are relatively certain an external change is afoot, it is better for both your mental health and your career to find a way to escape.

18. Derailment by Sub-Unit Arrogance

> "Those dumb SOBs at headquarters don't know their ass from a hole in the ground."—*Member of a derailed, disbanded work group*

Hazard 81: Building a Team by Demeaning Other Teams

Building the identity and motivation of a sub-unit of a larger organization by its self-perceived superiority to other units, or the organization as a whole, is an extremely hazardous practice. Thumbing your nose and boasting of your unit's superiority can lead to derailment for both your employees and your entire sub-unit. Derailment by sub-unit arrogance is becoming more common in an era of serial mergers as the derailment of Howard and many of his staff members exemplifies.

Howard's Mistake: The Folly of Building a Team on a Foundation of Animosity to Outsiders

A corporate vice president of an international pharmaceutical firm asked two of us to work with Howard and his staff to help develop a more cohesive and organizationally supportive team. He was concerned that Howard, the director of a somewhat autonomous sub-unit, and some of his key employees were not, as he stated it, "good corporate citizens." Howard was a reluctant client but eventually agreed to let us conduct a series of diagnostic interviews with his staff and facilitate just one group team-building session. The interviews revealed a high degree of anger and animosity toward the parent company because Howard's unit had been acquired and didn't welcome the imposition of new standards and policies. The acquisition occurred two years earlier but the strong resentment lingered.

Howard's opening comments at the group session crystallized our perception of the group's basic problem. He started the meeting with a diatribe, berating both his boss and the corporate staff for their poor strategy, lack of vision, and finally, for sending us out to work with his team. He told us not to take it personally but it was "just another one of those corporate decisions that didn't make sense." Even with that demotivating start, we actually had a semi-productive session. There were some issues within the team that didn't involve their relationship with the parent corporation and we helped them sort some of them out. Before leaving, we had a private session with Howard and shared our perception that the real problem was rooted in his attempt to build his team around animosity to the parent firm and that it wouldn't result in a good outcome for either he or his employees. He didn't buy it, wished us well, and showed us the door.

This was one instance where we were not excited by being proven correct. He was talented and had some very good people on his team. However, the predictable outcome occurred a few months after our visit. Howard was terminated and his replacement had no patience for working with people he described as "malcontents," and many of his former team members joined him in the external labor market.

We take careful notes during diagnostic interviews and examples of the kind of statements we heard from Howard and his group members were—"We're better than them"—"Those dumb SOBs at headquarters don't know their ass from a hole in the ground" and—"They have no concept of what's it's like in the real world. I ignore their advice and do it my way." In most cases the focus on the system or "them" was accompanied by a "him" or "her" indicating animosity not just to an organizational entity, but to a specific person. Howard's organization wasn't unique. I've heard these kinds of comments from other organizations. In some cases they were simply a short-term process of venting and, although not professional, they did no lasting harm. However, if they become a pattern and are used to bond and differentiate a team from other parts of an organization, they are far from harmless. They are preludes to derailment.

Hazard 82: Fostering Animosity Toward Higher Organizational Units

The Wages of Insubordination: General McChrystal's Derailment

The most public example of derailment by bonding a team around individual and hierarchical animosity involved General Stanley McChrystal, former commander of U.S. and NATO Coalition Forces in Afghanistan. In a speech, he labeled Vice President Biden's strategy of counter-terrorism as short sighted and by implication not compatible with his own approach. A year later, an in-depth profile exposed the intense degree of hostility and disrespect he and his staff held for supposedly collegial leaders such as Vice President Biden, Afghanistan Ambassador Eikenberrry, Special Representative Holbrooke, and National Security Advisor James Jones. Comments by his team also indicated McChrystal had shared his poor impression of his commander in chief, President Obama (Hastings 2010). After reviewing the article and meeting with McChrystal, Obama promptly fired him. General McChrystal paid a steep price for his sub-unit arrogance. It cost him his job and impacted the careers of his staff.

Derailment by mutual bonding around animosity to another organizational entity, higher management, or specific individuals is dangerous, not only for the leader, but also for staff members who can become seduced by the process. Internal transfers are blocked because group members are stereotyped as trouble makers. Organizational decision makers have long and unforgiving memories of those who, in the past, mocked and dismissed their ideas and contributions. Comments with the general theme of, "You wouldn't want to have 'him' on your team; he was one 'her' guys," are representative of this.

Hazard 83: Over-Identification with a High-Performing Sub-System

The Vulnerability of High-Performing Sub-Systems

Sub-units that actually out-perform their peer groups offer no immunity to derailment. In his pioneering research on qualities that separate truly high-performing systems from their competitors, Vaill (1982) articulated three differentiating qualities: laser-like focus, emotional attachment, and a major investment of time. He also discovered a paradoxical fact that explains the derailment of some very talented, albeit, non-team playing leaders. High-performing sub-systems are a threat to the primary system; they resist control, form impenetrable boundaries, and set their own standards. They are not just "curve raisers," they threaten, and often thumb their noses at the overall organizational culture.

Leaders of high-performing sub-systems lead hazardous, schizophrenic organizational lives. They are driven by the self-directed traits that motivate and stimulate entrepreneurs, yet they want to remain part of large organizations. To survive, they must navigate a mine field of bureaucratic control while leading rebellious, but high-performing, sub-systems. They give themselves and those who report to them mixed messages concerning autonomy and control. This not only endangers their own mental health, but often puts them on a slippery slope that leads to the formation of a team whose identity is based on its insubordination and enmity toward the primary system.

The Wake-Up Call of a High-Performing Leader

Unless very careful, high-performing sub-systems are susceptible to derailment that often comes as a sad and surprising wake-up call to the leader. That was the situation with Cindy. She was always an outlier. As an undergraduate she was a brilliant student, excelling in math and physics. These were not subjects where women traditionally excelled or were always welcomed. Because of her performance and uniqueness, she was invited to join groups such as her school's math club and the student/faculty astrophysics society. She declined, just as she declined invitations to join social sororities and scholastic honor societies. She cultivated a small group of fellow outliers who enjoyed their separation and formed an identity by poking fun at the "normal" groups.

She continued to both excel and remain isolated in graduate school where she breezed through a Ph.D. program in applied mathematics. A portion of her doctoral research dealt with the use of statistical techniques to predict successful recruiting outcomes. As a part of this process she spent a summer as an intern in an HR department where I also had a brief affiliation and we have remained in distant contact.

Upon graduation she passed on several faculty offers at prestigious universities. As a confirmed self-directed outlier, she didn't want to go through the conforming hoops required to achieve tenure. Instead, she chose to ply her trade in the world of commerce, securing a position as an individual contributor to a small group focused on developing statistically oriented software for government and military applications.

She wasn't an individual contributor long. Her talent and hard work caught the attention of a top manager and, after some negotiation, she agreed to head up a small independent group of advanced software developers. She did too well. Her group was stunningly successful at software development and stunningly unsuccessful at corporate citizenship.

Cindy was blind to the reality that despite her unit's performance, their perceived arrogance, disregard for corporate processes, and lack of concern for integrating their product into the corporate strategy was a brew that was lethal to the unit's survival. Her wake-up call came when her protective top manager retired and was replaced by an ambitious, intolerant careerist who reaped the political currency of breaking up her organization. They were dispersed to other software groups. Cindy left the firm and ended up as a university faculty member after all.

Hazard 84: Loyalty and Commitment to Own Work: Indifference to the Organization as a Whole

The Self-Initiated Derailment of an Outlier: The Saga of Seymour Cray

Since high-performing sub-systems have a limited shelf-life and seem doomed to be eventually absorbed into more manageable, but also more mediocre primary systems, the seduction of leading high-performing sub-systems can lead to a series of self-initiated derailments. This was the blessing and curse of legendary computer design engineer Seymour Cray.

Part of Engineering Research Associates, a small entrepreneurial start-up that became absorbed into the UNIVAC division of the Sperry Rand Corporation, Cray chafed at the bureaucracy and along with some former colleagues formed Control Data Corporation under the leadership of William Norris. With a small group of engineers, Cray lead a high-performing sub-system that designed the first fully transistorized and, at the time, largest computer in existence. Control Data predictably morphed into a large system, and once again Cray felt constrained by the structure and control.

In order to keep him in the primary system, but re-create the high-performing environment of the past, Control Data built a small isolated research facility in Seymour's home town, Chippewa Falls, Wisconsin. Working in this small town with a very small, very talented staff, Cray designed the 6600, the world's fastest supercomputer throughout most of the 1960s.

Once again, the practical imperatives of corporate politics, strategies, and budgets caught up with Seymour and he resigned from the board of directors. He decided, for what turned out to be for a short time, to remain with Control Data before starting his own firm. In a statement that clearly articulates the paradoxical relationship between a high-performing sub-system and a primary system he indicated that his decision was based on dedication to his own work and not out of commitment or loyalty to the corporation (Jensen 2013).

Hazard 85: Naïve Sub-Unit Loyalty

Derailment by naïve loyalty to a sub-unit is most often the result of new, inexperienced employees who are blind to the reality of the corporate power and decision-making structure. They are unduly influenced by more senior, often jaded and cynical sub-unit managers. The case of Belinda and the computer decision provides a classic example.

The Derailment of an Impressionable Intern

Belinda was a summer intern in the Southern California branch of a training and research firm, headquartered on the east coast. She was working on a master's degree in organizational development and the firm had plans to offer her a full-time position upon graduation. The California branch was one of three in the U.S. and there was a fledgling European operation in Brussels as well. The firm had reached such a size, complexity, and need to better coordinate, that a decision was made to link the branches through a common computer system.

The branches were historically semi-autonomous, and within each branch, consultants pursued their individual specialties. Every employee had a desktop computer but no attempt was made to standardize either hardware or software. The majority of computers in the California branch were Apple Macintoshes. The other branches had a mix, with the majority favoring the Microsoft Windows variety. A task force was formed with representatives from each branch, and after a lengthy period of deliberation, the decision was made to replace the Macs and design an integrated system using Windows-based machines.

Belinda's boss, William, the branch manager, was a talented consultant, but a salty, crusty curmudgeon as a leader. He was a year away from retirement, and those with experience knew his bark was much worse than his bite and not to take his outbursts seriously. Unfortunately, Belinda didn't get the message. She joined the branch the week after the computer decision was made and, although the logic was clearly explained and the branch had participated in the deliberations, most liked their Macs and there was the normal amount of grousing, but to most, it wasn't a major issue.

William wasn't heavily invested in the decision, but true to form, he lost no opportunity to complain about the arbitrary decision making of top management and the burgeoning bureaucracy that diminished employee choice and freedom. Belinda worked closely with William throughout the summer and didn't have the experience or perspective to discount his complaints and came to believe that uncaring top management had forced a bad decision on a helpless sub-unit.

The branch was very impressed with Belinda's work and wanted to hire her when she graduated the following spring. In order to reward her efforts and further their chances of landing her upon graduation, the branch management committee decided to include her—a lowly intern—in the firm's annual celebratory planning and award meeting. It was a combination pep rally, dispensation of awards and recognition for goal achievement, announcement of plans for the coming year, and celebratory party. The venue was a plush resort in Florida.

During the opening dinner, Belinda ended up at a table with a group that included the vice president of administration, who, among other duties, was in charge of the new computer system. She, conditioned by William's outbursts and misconstruing her role as one of defending branch autonomy and fighting corporate bureaucracy, unloaded on him. Public chastisement in that festive environment from an inexperienced intern over a decision that the firm tried very hard to make participative, was not what he wanted to hear. In order to stem the negative flow, he tabled the issue and arranged to meet with her over breakfast.

He included the firm's president in that breakfast meeting and after patiently explaining the process for making the decision and the logic of the choice, thought the subject was closed. He was wrong. That evening the participants were divided into four sub-groups and asked to comment on the next year's goals and raise any issues that might get in the way of their achievement. Based on previous years, it was expected to be a positive exercise and facilitate ownership. When Belinda's sub-group reported the highlights of their discussion to the entire group, the spokesperson said positive things, but also indicated there was one lingering issue that required airing. Rather that summarize it herself, she asked Belinda to speak.

Belinda, again, made the same angry speech, naïvely unaware that she was both violating a cultural norm and earning the wrath of top management. When she returned to California William called her into his office and fired her. He had received a phone call from the president directing that action. Rather than owning up to his complicity in conditioning her naïve sub-unit arrogant behavior, he remained in character, telling her that she was correct in her confrontation and he was just following orders.

The lesson for sub-unit managers who enjoy making derisive comments about other units or top management is that young, impressionable employees may take them more seriously than intended, and, like Belinda, make it their mission to right the perceived wrong. If you are a new, inexperienced employee, the lesson is to withhold judgment on disparaging, states rights oriented comments until you better understand the system and the motivation of the person making those comments.

Perspective and Advice

- Never build a team around hostility and sarcasm directed at other organizational units or individuals. It's a fragile, self-serving, and ultimately, unsupportable foundation. It can and will crumble.
- No matter what your impression, never publicly denigrate your boss to those who work for you. If you want to challenge your leader, do it directly. It's cowardly to do it second-hand through your employees. There is no upside and the odds are significant that it will get back to him or her. What goes around comes around, and you are also giving license to your employees to do unto you what you have done onto your boss.

- Denigrating the leader or decisions made higher in the system is a seductive practice. Guard against it. It may add spice to organizational life and feel affirming to mock and defame others but it will never end well.
- If your boss is addicted to this strategy, you have the basic psychological "fight or flight" option. If you choose "fight" you can use direct confrontation and try and help him understand the eventual consequences, or you can simply abstain from negativism and blaming and counter with positive comments. Most who practice upward bashing are ego-involved in their misdirected tactics and will be threatened by direct confrontation. You may, however, be surprised at the power of abstinence and positive comments. You may also find some closet allies among your peers. The "flight" option requires finding a different boss or leaving. If you want to remain in the organization, finding an internal transfer, even if it involves dropping down a level, is the most viable choice.
- Creating a self-contained organization that performs exceptionally well but is arrogant, flaunts bureaucratic processes, adopts a "we're the best, so we're immune from the rules" culture, is a blueprint for derailment. The primary system can and will strike back. Too many talented and creative leaders are shocked by the inevitable wake-up call when their high-performing sub-system is broken up and they are left hanging. Managers who have supported and complied with the constraints of the organizational culture have little sympathy or job options for mavericks that, regardless of their successes, have lived outside the rules.
- If you are a leader who is invested in creating a high-performing system using Vaill's blend of time, feeling, and focus, and want to remain a long-term player in the overall organization, it is essential that you work exceptionally hard to maintain your credibility and support in the primary system. You must resist the addictive seduction of arrogance and superiority. It's a relatively short-term rush and it will only lead to damage to your employees and your own career prospects.
- If, like Seymour Cray, you attempt to continually create internal skunk work—like safe havens—you'll be disappointed. The primary system will always prevail and temporary systems will ultimately crumble or simply morph into another "normal" entity.

Part VII

Dysfunctional Traits

The three chapters in this section discuss and provide help in overcoming dysfunctional traits that can lead to derailment. There is a dark and dangerous side to charismatic leadership that can both damage people and cause entire systems to come off the tracks. People derail by irrelevance because their skills and leadership styles are not of value to today's organizations. Withdrawing from the demanding tasks of leadership and not engaging in productive relationships with employees is the formula for leadership derailment by avoidance.

Part VII Chapter Summary

The Three Categories of Dysfunctional Trait Risks and How to Navigate Them

Derailment Risks	*What to Do About Them*
Chapter 19: Charisma: Inability to modify the "rightness" of a vision or values. Delusion of invincibility and low tolerance for dissension.	Seek and accept external evaluation of the validity of your vision and openness to feedback. Don't become a victim of the adulation of followers.
Chapter 20: Irrelevance: Skills, style, and values no longer fit the current organizational culture.	Engage in an honest self-assessment of the fit between your competencies and those valued by your organization and have the courage and discipline to make changes.
Chapter 21: Avoidance: Unwillingness to authentically engage with employees and escape into non-essential diversions.	If you lack the energy or enthusiasm to engage in a helping relationship with your employees seek help. Even if you have the connections to hang on to your job, you're not doing yourself or your organization any good by attempting to survive.

19. Derailment by Charisma

> "The three most charismatic leaders in this century inflicted more suffering on the human race than almost any trio in history: Hitler, Stalin, and Mao." —*Peter Drucker*

Charismatic leadership is a good news, bad news, very bad news proposition. The good news is that charismatic leaders have the potential to energize their followers, bond them around a compelling future vision, and enable them to overcome seemingly impossible obstacles to achieve that vision. The bad news is that even "good" charismatic leaders are susceptible to self-aggrandizement, intolerance of dissention, and the creation of cult-like followers. The very bad news is that "bad" charismatic leaders can cause death and destruction.

Hazard 86: Completely Trusting a Charismatic Leader

People such as Mohandas Gandhi, John F. Kennedy, Jack Welch, Winston Churchill and Martin Luther King have been described as "good" charismatic leaders. On the dark side, Adolf Hitler, Charles Manson, David Koresh, Osama Bin Laden, and Jim Jones displayed exceptionally strong charismatic characteristics (Welch 2013). When someone describes a leader to me as charismatic, I become wary and red flags temper my judgment. Considering the risks of even the good ones, I much prefer working with leaders who have a low to moderate quotient of charismatic traits.

Characteristics of Charismatic Leaders and Their Followers

The concept was initially articulated by German sociologist Max Weber, who also developed and advocated the theory of bureaucracy.

Charismatic leadership was the first of his three types of legitimate rule (Best 2002, 12). Weber described charismatic leadership as a process where a leader influences not by traditional authority systems but on followers' perceptions that the leader is endowed with the gift of divine inspiration or supernatural powers. Over time, at least in the world of business, Weber's conceptualization has been modified, but charismatic leaders are still seen as heroic and, often, invincible.

Whether the context is business, politics, or cults, charismatic leaders have similar effects on their followers. They trust in the "rightness" of the leader's future vision and tend to accept very challenging goals and take personal risks to make that vision a reality. They unconditionally accept the leader's beliefs and goals. They emulate and have strong affection for him. All varieties of charismatic leaders, in turn, also have similar traits. They are visionary, have superb communication skills, and lose no opportunity to articulate their vision and promote themselves. They have no self-doubt or moral conflict and are willing to sacrifice themselves and their followers for the "cause." Again, there is good news and bad news. They find ways to empower others who buy into their vision. They also find ways to disempower and severely punish those who don't.

Hazard 87: Membership in a Business Cult

A Clash of Cultures: The Predictable Demise of an Organizational Cult

Most business organizations are not cults or religions. Some, however, have similar characteristics along with the requisite charismatic leader. I experienced the seduction of one cult-like business organization first hand. Even as an outsider who knew better, I found it difficult to resist the emotional attraction of the religious fervor that dominated this business. The leader and most of the "born again" followers eventually and predictably derailed. They came off the tracks, not because of the performance of this small regional consumer loan business, but because of a cultural clash with the much larger and worldlier organization that acquired their firm. Even without the triggering acquisition, the business was fated to fail. Cults are insular, closed systems that rigorously adhere to their own norms and scoff at those of the outside world. In an era of political correctness, federal regulations such as the Equal Opportunity Laws, and litigious customers, the business was predestined to fail.

I was a member of the acquiring organization's acquisition team. On our first visit, we were introduced to the management group and, unlike any of our previous experiences, were initially engaged by a lengthy prayer, led by the firm's president. He prayed for a successful merger—he never owned up the fact that it wasn't a merger but an acquisition. The prayer ended with a strong plea for profits, interspersed with "Amens" from the local managers.

The firm had a church-like quality and probably contrarily to the law and certainly against the acquiring firm's policies, they prayed and liberally interspersed Southern Baptist teachings into their meetings. It was an exclusive congregation: there were no African Americans or women in any managerial role. There was a hierarchical "priesthood" with the president, who was also the firm's founding father, at the top. He was deified by the employees and responded by dispensing gifts (a year-end bonus and the promise of a promotion) to those he deemed worthy. Central to the culture was the belief that profit was supreme and the requirement that personal needs be subordinated to an overarching organizational loyalty. The ultimate reward was continued employment (remaining in the cult) and the honor of being part of the team (avoiding excommunication).

The firm had many characteristics of a religious cult: a regular Saturday morning meeting (service) with stories of sales and quota achievements (testimonies) followed by applause, handshakes, affirming smiles (fellowship of believers), and a pep talk (sermon) by the founding father. There were rewards (gift certificates for restaurants and the local Walmart) dispensed to those who had done an extra good job, and symbols (watches and other trinkets correlated in value to years of membership in the congregation). The organization did not have a company song, but it did have a number of mottos and slogans that were tacked to office walls and even placed in full face-high view over the urinals in the men's room.

The good news was that this unique, self-contained business cult worked exceedingly well before it was acquired. Profits grew, the founding father became very wealthy, and the employees were generally happy. The bad news was that the acquiring company imposed its policies, including compliance with federal employment laws, and the founding father along with most of his top disciples derailed because their self esteem and sense of purpose were hard wired to the cult and they were unwilling to change.

After an initial "hands off," honeymoon phase, the acquiring organization's vice president of operations, not noted for his cultural sensitivity, ordered an end to prayer. "This is a business organization, not a church," was his oft quoted logic. He also required salary integration with the parent company's much more liberal structure, payment of overtime for non-exempt employees who were required to attend Saturday pep rallies, and implementation of the company's affirmative action program. In a final symbolic act of cultural destruction, he personally removed the slogan-bearing posters from above the urinals.

During the next year the cult leader and the vice president engaged in an increasingly counterproductive organizational game of bait and switch. The cult leader, along with his disciples, would publicly pledge compliance with corporate policies and privately violate and scoff at them. In testimony to the pettiness of the game, the above-the-urinal posters played a central role. They would be removed during corporate visits and re-attached when the visitors left. In an unannounced visit, the vice president discovered them during a coffee break, prompting an angry confrontation resulting in the founding father's on-the-spot decision to retire. Because of their reputations for dogmatic non-compliance, most of his top disciples were eventually terminated. The founding father retired to live off of his millions, but he left his followers with nothing more than their meager severance pay. There were no profit sharing or stock options in that cult.

Aside from the inevitable unraveling of self-contained, insular business cults in today's environment, there are two additional lessons to be learned. The first is that the self-centeredness and megalomania of charismatic leaders allows them to take care of themselves, untroubled by any responsibility for the welfare of their followers. The president moved to an oceanfront estate on a South Carolina island and left his followers high and dry in Georgia with no pensions, few assets, and no viable employment options.

The second lesson is for followers. Never put your self esteem, sense of purpose and value system in the hands of a charismatic leader. As much as you may want to please him, be like him, and adopt his values, it is a bad bargain. He can, and often will, betray your trust and leave you stranded.

Why Charismatic Leaders Derail

Charismatic leaders derail for two reasons. The first is that they fall victim to their own megalomania. Seduced by the trust and adoration of their followers, they are casualties to a self-belief in their "rightness," and, without corrective feedback, make decisions that result in their own and often their organization's derailment. Napoleon's ego-driven 1812 decision to march to Moscow is a historical example. The result was the destruction of the French army. A business example was the stubborn adherence by William Norris, the founder and charismatic CEO of Control Data Corporation, to tenaciously cling to reliance on large, mainframe computers as a primary source of revenue (Hayes 2002). Not heeding advice to switch to personal and business computers was a decision that contributed to that corporation's demise and the loss of thousands of jobs.

The second reason for charismatic leader derailment is that threats to their self esteem and carefully constructed, unchallenged paradigms of reality trigger paranoia and self and system destruction. Jim Jones poisoned his followers with Kool-Aid and shot himself. Hitler destroyed a country, left a legacy of evil morality and committed suicide. David Koresh led his followers to death in a fire. Enron went belly-up, employees lost their retirement savings, Ken Lay and Jeff Skilling were sentenced to prison, and Arthur Andersen, lost its credibility and ceased operating as an auditing firm. Although Bernie Madoff doesn't come off as displaying the galvanizing personality of a stereotypical charismatic leader, investors in his long-running Ponzi scheme trusted the "rightness" of his investment skills and saw him as a larger-than-life purveyor of wealth. When it all imploded, Madoff was destroyed along with the funds of many follower/investors.

Transformation: The Tame Cousin of Charisma

Transformational leadership is a concept first popularized by leadership expert James MacGregor Burns (1978) and later refined by Bernard Bass (1994). It is a more moderate, organizationally palatable version of Weber's original notion of charismatic leadership. Leaders are not perceived as having supernatural powers or divine characteristics. They do, however, have the ability to provide inspiration and the skills to articulate and stimulate acceptance and commitment to a galvanizing future vision.

Transformational leadership is often contrasted with transactional leadership. Transformational leaders are compelled to change the status quo by highlighting problems within the current system and formulating a compelling vision of what a new organization could be. Transactional leaders focus on promoting stability rather than promoting change. They lead by clarifying and monitoring existing processes and cultural norms.

Hazard 88: Premature Transformational Leadership

Too often hard-wired transformational leaders attempt abrupt cultural change before organizations are ready and when the real need is for a transactional approach. Their style is driven more by their compulsion to lead a transformation than the organization's need for stability. This imposed transformation by a change driven leader can be path to derailment as was the case with Dr. Phyllis.

When Ill-Timed Transformation Leads to Derailment: A Case Study

Dr. Phyllis Johnson was named president of a southern community college with a large regional market area. She was selected by a hastily formed search committee after her predecessor was forced to resign because of a combination of financial mismanagement—some called it stealing—and sexual harassment. Both transgressions came to a head at the same time, and he was rapidly evicted from office.

Dr. Phyllis, as she liked to be called, visualized herself as a transformational leader. Her previous role was as a curriculum consultant to public school systems. Prior to that, she had a number of administrative roles in a state university. This was her first top management job. The politics, bureaucracy, and petty academic quarrels of her past positions left her frustrated and determined to preside over a transformed educational institution.

Due to the departed president's mismanagement there was confusion over the administration of a new remote facility. Department heads ignored policy and freelanced in regard to curriculum, marketing, hiring, and budget compliance. The college badly needed discipline, structure and stability. The last thing they needed was a time consuming workshop on visioning or an out-of-context, mistimed experiential team-building session complete with blind trust walks, interpersonal disclosure, and feedback exercises. The organization needed a heavy dose of transactional leadership but Dr. Phyllis tried to apply even heavier, ill-timed transformational leadership tools. The school wasn't ready for transformation and, even if it was, she had no real experience either with the tools or credibility as a transformational leader.

One year into her tenure things had significantly deteriorated. Teacher morale had declined and the curriculum remained a Byzantine, illogical mess, confusing to both faculty and students. Relationships between faculty and administrative staff, fragile under the best of circumstances, were exceptionally strained, paralyzing any serious efforts for coordination and planning. Her persistent, amateurish efforts to rapidly transform the organization only made things worse, spawning confusion and mistrust. The more she pressed for transformation, the more it was apparent that the real need was for stability and transactional leadership.

I was retained by her board to conduct a survey of the faculty and staff to help both Dr. Phyllis and her board of advisors determine the true state of their community college's union. The results were worse than even the most pessimistic board member—the one who retained me—expected. Dr. Phyllis had a slim chance to keep her job, but, when the results were presented at a board meeting, she grew defensive and combative, arguing, not only with the survey conclusions, but also suggesting that the board itself needed radical transformation. She probably would have been fired but she acted first, resigned and followed her predecessor out the door.

Hazard 89: Transformation Overload

The Blessing and Curse of a Serial Transformational Leader

Unlike Dr. Phyllis, Curtis is an experienced and gifted transformational leader. His problem is that he can't stop transforming and give the organization a respite. He is a serial transformational leader, addicted to transforming organizational systems whether they need it or not.

He fits the classic description of a charismatic leader. He is a gifted communicator excelling in both verbal and non-verbal skills. He has an unshakable faith in his ability to visualize and stimulate commitment to a future vision. The problem is that if he is around an organization too long he burns out his followers, loses interest in leading, and derails.

In his early career, he conceptualized himself as a turnaround expert.

19. Derailment by Charisma

He would accept jobs in small technology firms or divisions of larger companies that were struggling with product development and marketing. He seldom stayed in one job longer than two years, sometimes much less. He was almost always successful and he almost always derailed. Once he had everyone on the same page, committed to a positive and achievable plan of action, he'd abandon that page and formulate another. In existential philosophical terms, he was always in the process of becoming, never being. He would derail because the organization needed stability to digest the results of their transformation and he was incapable of providing it.

He wisely concluded he was unfit to ever live with the results of his transformational efforts in one company. He has found an unusual vocational niche but one that fits. He is a consultant to a large international consulting firm. He contracts with their "change management" function, works with their clients in visioning and strategy formulation and gets out of the way of any implementation phase. The firm has offered him a job, but he is insightful enough to know that organizational permanence would be incompatible with his transformational addiction.

Perspective and Advice

- There is a dark side to charismatic leadership. Without moral grounding and external monitoring, it can evolve into a destructive, cult-like culture that, when the leader inevitably derails, the careers and sometimes the lives of organizational members are destroyed.
- If you work in a business or non-profit organization with a charismatic leader and cult-like norms, beware: the leader won't hesitate to sacrifice you to achieve her goals. As was the case with the small consumer lending firm, the leader will convert you to a style of behavior and leadership that works only inside her idiosyncratic self-contained organization. When it implodes, you can be left with no financial resources and employment skills and values that won't fit anywhere else. Difficult though it may be and value-conflicted though you may feel, get out while you can. The organization will unravel and the charismatic leader will tend to her own agenda which most likely won't include you.
- If you are a budding transformational leader and self-actualize by creating compelling future visions and inspiring others to drop the

status quo and move into a more exciting future, be careful where you ply your trade. Organizations must be ready for fundamental transformation and many leaders have derailed by pushing too hard, too fast. Effective transformational leadership is only possible when built on a foundation of stability. If the organization needs structure and stability, build that first through transactional leadership.

- If you are in a position to retain a leader, check references carefully. Beware of serial transformational leaders. They are never satisfied with single or incremental transformations and, unless controlled, will drive their organizations into a frenzied jumble of multiple visions, values and missions. They can be extremely useful but need to be constrained, either through a short-term consulting relationship or a firm plan to step aside and ply their trade in a different part of your organization during implementation.

20. Derailment by Irrelevance

> "All of a sudden somebody hands you a slip of paper, they have you into HR with your boss and say, 'We don't need you anymore.' That's rough." —*Derailed middle manager*

Lawrence Peter's bestselling book, *The Peter Principle* (1969) captured the organizational tenor of the times with its central theme that employees in hierarchal organizations tend to raise to the level of their incompetence. In Peter's time, organizations were large and bureaucratic. The old psychological employment contract was in full effect: people signed up for a long-term career, there were no substantial layoffs, and tenure was rewarded with promotion. Although somewhat of a spoof, the book struck a chord. It was discussed around corporate water coolers, spawned a board game, and even stimulated a BBC TV series. The reason was that there were many incompetent people in many excessively layered and over-bureaucratized organizations. As time marched on, these incompetent people didn't necessarily derail; they just festered in place, protected by the inefficient bureaucratic cocoon they helped perpetuate.

Peter's concept of an incompetent "hierarchiology" was undone by the era of re-engineering, globalization, technical advances, outsourcing, and massive waves of layoffs and downsizing. The old psychological employment contract died and was replaced by a new reality. People were no longer long-term assets to be nurtured and kept on the payroll for a lifetime career. They were short-term costs and, unless they possessed skills of immediate value, were discarded; derailed by the dawn of the new psychological contract.

Hazard 90: Inability to Adjust to the New Psychological Employment Contract

Polar Responses to the New Reality: The Tale of Gilbert and Freddie

Gilbert and his best friend Freddie lived in a small North Carolina town. They both worked in a plant that manufactured furniture. Gilbert was in woodworking and finishing and Freddie was worked in assembly and fabric installation. The plant had been a fixture in their town for 40 years and, aside from a few retail operations and a small mom and pop cement business, was the primary employer and reason for the town's existence.

They graduated from high school in the same class. Freddie was the star football jock and, a year after graduation, married the most popular girl in his class. Gilbert was the better student and, after a few years of rather boring bachelorhood, ended up marrying a practical nurse who, three days a week, made the long commute to a Charlotte hospital. In many ways Freddie and Gilbert were the same. They both drove pick-up trucks, were emotionally invested in their growing families, dutifully but not very spiritually attended the local Methodist church, enjoyed more than an occasional after work round of beers, and cheered for the Carolina Panthers. They weren't exactly red necks and the town wasn't exactly Mayberry, and they weren't exactly happy, but all three dimensions came close.

They liked their jobs and, under the unstated but clearly understood terms of the old psychological employment contract, assumed that if they kept their noses clean and worked hard, they could keep those jobs until they retired. They were in their early 40s when the peak wave of offshoring—moving manufacturing to lower cost Asian locations, closing factories, and laying off long-term workers—really hit the North Carolina furniture industry.

Gilbert, through the coaching and prompting of his more worldly and networked wife, saw what was coming and got ready. He sold his Panthers season tickets and used the money to help with tuition and the extra time to study. He curtailed his beer stops and shifted his evening time from cable TV to online courses and textbooks. He adjusted his work schedule so that he could commute to a community college where he was enrolled in a program offering certification in aircraft maintenance and mechanics.

It was a rigorous curriculum and required a fundamental change in lifestyle from his previous pseudo-Mayberry, laid-back existence, but he conjured up the energy and commitment and got through it.

Freddie did nothing. With his head buried deeply in the sand—or, more accurately, the North Carolina red clay—he, when he thought about it at all, hoped the Asian job exodus would stop and things would return to normal. Normal never came back. With little notice and even littler severance pay, the factory closed and 150 people lost their jobs. Gilbert wasn't one of them. Three months earlier he quit and took a job in a booming aircraft repair and maintenance operation in Greensboro.

Today Gilbert is making more money than at the factory, has better benefits, and is employed in a thriving business. He and his wife are spending some of that money on gas because he is commuting to Greensboro and she to Charlotte, but overall life is good. Freddie found he had no skills that fit the demands of the new labor market. He remains in what is left of his hometown, drinks too much, has gained too much weight, and works part-time for minimum wage as a loader in the mom and pop cement works.

The clear lesson from the tale of Gilbert and Freddie is to avoid derailment by irrelevance by taking the time and making the effort to develop and continually hone skills that are valued in the marketplace. Complacency is the ally of derailment by irrelevancy. Think of Freddie and don't let it happen to you.

Hazard 91: Failure to Develop and Maintain Marketable Skills

The Middle Manager: An Endangered Species

In the old psychological contract, middle managers served dual roles as communicators between those at the top and the front line workers and as enforcers and role models of the corporate culture. With the advent of personal computers the top and the bottom could communicate directly without the intermediary role of a middle manager. Corporations no longer bought into the family metaphor and an integrating, sustaining, long-term culture took a back seat to short-term profits and disposable employees. The result was a massive derailment of middle managers in almost all organizations. They were not derailed because of incompetence, but simply because they were not needed and irrelevant to the needs of the organization. The structural organizational legacy of this wholesale derailment is flatter organizations, much larger spans of managerial control, and personal computers on nearly all desks. The human toll is derailed managers, seduced by skills no longer of value to their past employer and not transferable to any other, and salary requirements based on past tenure and not the current external market. Too many, like Malcolm became demoralized, lacked the energy or aptitude to learn marketable skills, and simply give up.

Hazard 92: Having Values and Know-How of Use to Only One Organization

Surrendering to Irrelevance: A Sad Example

Malcolm's last official job title was "Manager of Logistics"—early in his career it was called "Production Control." Prior to being washed away by a tsunami of corporate layoffs, he spent twelve years in a facility that manufactured disc drives and printers. In addition to production control management he possessed the special skill of finding ways to get things through the corporate system. If you wanted a purchase requisition approved that was out of policy, Malcolm was the man to see. If you needed to find a way to subcontract a component, but outsourcing was not in the operational plan, Malcolm knew what levers to pull. He knew all the forms, all the procedures and all the ways to get things through the bureaucratic controls. I ran into him when an internal client needed help finding funding for a team-building workshop. Malcolm found a way and was a very engaged participant in the session.

Malcolm was the victim of two dimensions of derailment by irrelevance. First, his job was eliminated by technology. Scheduling, component procurement, logistics and coordination with sales was done by computer or outsourced. Like many middle managers, Malcolm was essentially replaced by personal computers. Middle managers also served a second function; one in which Malcolm excelled. Like sergeants in the army, they were the repository of wisdom, process know-how, and keepers of the informal system. De-layering, organizational cultures with primary focus on short-term profits, and the unfolding of the new psychological employment contract eroded the value of this second middle management role.

Similar to the experience of many middle managers, Malcolm floundered in the new reality-based labor market. His skill base was forged to be of value only to a single employer and was not transferable to other firms. No one cared about his ability to get things through his previous company's system. Without the requisite technical skills, no one valued his ability to personally coordinate complex logistical issues. Complicating matters was his salary. Due to old psychological contract "wage for age" compensation practices, he was significantly over-priced in the external labor market.

Malcolm lost his identity, his sense of purpose, and his confidence. He grew depressed and had no interest in retooling his skills and competing with younger, lower-priced, and more technically competent job seekers. He simply gave up and, when I last saw him was working weekends for an hourly wage as a sales clerk in a big box hardware outlet.

If you are a derailed middle manager don't follow the sad example of Malcolm. You'll feel much better about yourself if you pull out of your funk and acquire some new skills. There are many relatively stress-free venues available to learn marketable skills and, counter to the cliché, old dogs can, indeed, learn new tricks. Although unfortunately, age discrimination is alive and well, there are jobs out there and as the fictional Don Quixote proved, trying is always better than giving up.

If you know a derailed middle manager try to help him overcome his natural depression. Being pushed out of a career because skills that were once valued are no longer deemed relevant is a devastating experience. You don't have to be a trained therapist to engage in a helping relationship. However, if the situation calls for it, don't hesitate to recommend finding one.

Hazard 93: Inability to Drop a Command-and-Control Orientation

Unlike middle managers, senior leaders don't often derail because of a lack of marketable skills or technological irrelevance. They come off the relevancy track because their style doesn't fit the needs of contemporary organizations. The most common style mismatch is between top managers who are locked into a command-and-control style and organizations that require leaders who are oriented toward a helping and facilitating style.

In today's complex, post-layoff environment, organizations need leaders to help employees focus on customer service, recover from the trauma of layoffs and mergers, and remain engaged and committed to organizational excellence. The best employees have external options and are drawn to their organizations because of the work. They stay because they want to, not because they have to. Command-and-control is an artifact of the old psychological employment contract and leaders who can't drop it derail both because they alienate this new breed of employee, and are unable to help re-recruit those who have lost their motivation and enthusiasm.

I have found it very difficult to help hard core command-and-control leaders change their style. It requires a fundamental shift of mindset and an admission that the style and approach that got them where they are won't keep them there. Admitting personal irrelevancy is a hard pill for senior leaders to swallow.

While working with one top leader, I was puzzled by his one step backward, one step forward progress. What I discovered was that, even though a significant shift in style was necessary to prevent his derailment, two influential members of his board, themselves products of command-and-control conditioning, were negatively reinforcing any change. Hard as it is to change the style of previously successful top managers, it is even harder to change the messages sent by those who influence them. After a meeting with the board it was clear that they were reinforcing the wrong leadership style and even clearer that, despite my recommendation, they would continue. I terminated my engagement and the style-challenged leader continued his irrelevant, counterproductive behavior for another year before he finally took early retirement.

Hazard 94: A Dependency Relationship with One Company or Industry

The Demise of the Lint Heads

Derailment by irrelevance is not limited to the shrinking role of middle managers or the style mismatch of top executives; it is also endemic in certain industries. One telling example is the textile and apparel industries in North Carolina. According to a Duke University study (2012) in 1996 there were 2,153 textile and apparel plants in North Carolina that employed 233,715 people. A decade later, there had been a 40 percent decline in the number of plants—and a 65 percent decrease in employment. The trend has rapidly accelerated in the current decade. The landscape of rural North Carolina is littered with the gutted shells of abandoned textile plants.

The requirements for employment were a strong back, a good work ethic, and residency in a non-union state. Entire villages developed around textile manufacturing plants. They were managed by paternalistic owners who employed multi-generational members of the same families. The employees of these company mill towns called themselves "lint heads," and, although they figuratively "owed their souls to the company stores," they formed cohesive, seemingly contented cultural units. That culture was devastated when the lint heads were derailed by irrelevance.

The lint heads lived by labor cost and died by it. North Carolina is a Right to Work state which means that union membership is not a requirement for employment, and mill workers were willing to work for substantially less pay than their unionized colleagues to the north. They were derailed by outsourcing. Their relatively low pay was made irrelevant by the much lower pay for the same work in Asia. Similar to the fate of displaced middle managers, the lint heads and their brethren in related industries entered the labor market without the requisite skills. There were no jobs for hard-working, undereducated, non-union, low-tech manufacturing workers.

Perspective and Advice

- Whether it be an outdated middle management role, the inability to compete with lower paid workers, or leadership skills that don't fit the needs of the organization, derailment by irrelevance is alive and well. It's a tough, ruthless labor market out there and a basic tenant of the new psychological employment contract is not just "what have you done for me lately," but "what skills and competencies do you have that will make you relevant to the growth and profitability of my business?"
- The key to preventing derailment by irrelevance is the strength to subject yourself to an honest self-assessment and the courage to act on the results. In almost every situation, the skills and behaviors that got you where you are won't keep you there. Complacency is the enemy. Don't be seduced by success. Things will change and, in

order to be ready, you need to take action. Regardless of how well you think you're doing, if you aren't engaged in self-development, you are losing ground.
- For many, the path to relevance involves the difficult task of acquiring the technical skills demanded by the higher paying jobs in today's labor market. For those without the means or aptitude to acquire these relevant skills, it requires a fundamental change in life style and settling for a different type of employment. For leaders whose style doesn't fit the needs of their organizations it requires either an extremely difficult change in approach, moving back into a non-leadership role, or attempting to beat the odds by seeking another job that better fits their style.

21. Derailment by Avoidance

"You mistake me for someone who gives a damn."
—*Terminally disengaged leader*

Terminal disengagement is a tragic and toxic condition that occurs when employees simply stop caring and disengage from investing their creativity, commitment, and human spirit into their organizations. It's tragic because it withers away and deadens human spirit and work joy. It's toxic because it kills organizational productivity.

Hazard 95: Succumbing to Disengagement

There is an epidemic of employee disengagement among organizations. Criteria and methodologies vary but one comprehensive study (Crabtree 2013) provided a perspective of the magnitude of the problem when it reported that only 13 percent of worldwide employees were actively engaged. The U.S. and Canada had the highest percentage of engaged employees with a paltry 29 percent while 18 percent were actively disengaged. Disengagement is a classic form of avoidance. It can lead to physical derailment—as in losing a job—and it always leads to motivational derailment—the bodies may be there but the heads, hearts and spirits are gone. It's at its worst when disengaged employees work for disengaged leaders.

Hazard 96: Working for a Disengaged Leader

The Lame Leading the Lame: When Disengaged Employees Work for Disengaged Leaders

Wise organizations are deeply concerned and work hard to promote employee engagement. In today's competitive environment, fielding a workforce of lethargic, disengaged, uncaring employees will result in not just individual derailments, but eventual derailment of the organization itself. I and some colleagues were asked to help a medical supply firm help formulate a strategy to respond to a devastating employee satisfaction survey. The results indicated that employee satisfaction, trust and confidence in leadership, belief in the importance of their work, and feeling that individual contributions were valued had significantly deteriorated since a previous survey. Even more alarming, there was no difference by level; the top felt as bad as the bottom. In most satisfaction surveys there is a hierarchical effect where the higher you reside, the better you feel. In this case, aside from the new CEO and his three new henchmen, organizational leaders felt as bad as hourly employees.

It had been four years since the previous survey and, during that time, the organization had gone through two major downsizings and a traumatic change in top management—the long-time, very paternalistic CEO had been forced out and was replaced by a younger executive who viewed employees not as long-term assets to be developed and nurtured, but as short-term costs to be reduced as much as possible. About the only people who were happy were the new CEO and the three managers he brought along with him when he joined the firm.

Our first finding was that the CEO didn't really care about the survey results and seriously misjudged the impact of a disengaged workforce on his organization's future. We were retained by the HR director and it was clear that the CEO didn't really want us bringing up, what he called "fuzzy," issues. It turned out to be a very short assignment, which was okay with us—it's not fun or affirming to work where you aren't wanted. It turned out not to be so okay for the CEO, who, after a year of high key employee turnover and low financial results, was dismissed. In retrospect, dispensing with false humility, we could have helped him save his job and improve his organizational effectiveness.

Our second discovery was that the organization was suffering from a classic case of layoff survivor sickness. Research shows that most survivors of layoffs who felt betrayed by the shift from the old (as long as you perform and fit in you can keep your job) to the new (short term, what have you done for me lately is the name of the game) psychological employment contract, emerged with feelings of anger, distrust, fear, and in too many cases, depression (Noer, 2009). It was a certain recipe for the disengagement that was reflected in the survey.

Our final observation was that the firm needed empathetic leaders who could help employees process their feelings and rekindle trust and commitment. What it didn't need were self-absorbed, disengaged leaders, wallowing in their own issues and unable to respond to the needs of their employees. In a sad, but telling moment of honesty, one formerly powerful executive we worked with during our short assignment, responded to a request to meet with his employees with the defining statement of a failed, disengaged leader, "You mistake me for someone who gives a damn."

Hazard 97: Self-Absorption

Characteristics of Terminally Disengaged Leaders

In my work with survivors of downsizings I encountered several terminally disengaged leaders. Most eventually lost their jobs or were relegated to insignificant holding patterns before retiring. While still occupying leadership roles, they had, however, made a bad situation worse and hindered their organizations' recoveries. They have four defining characteristics.

Something happened that deeply wounded and disabled them. It could be, as in the case of the executive who didn't give a damn, surviving a downsizing and discovering that, although he had kept his job, he hadn't retained his status and influence. It could be, as was the case with another client, facing the reality of his plateaued career and coming to the existential conclusion that the climb wasn't worth it and he had squandered his work life.

The primary coping mechanisms are withdrawal, self-absorption, isolation, and avoiding responsible, other-centered leadership. It's the opposite of the cliché "When the going gets tough, the tough get going." For terminally disengaged leaders it's "When the going gets tough, weak leaders with character flaws fold, turn inward and aren't there for their people."

They aren't happy or productive and the longer they stay in a leadership role the unhappier and less productive they become. Unfortunately, many, based on their level in the company and internal connections, stay far too long. The price of their extended tenure is ultimately paid by their employees who desperately need proactive, helpful, engaged leadership.

When they inevitably derail, they are greatly relieved and, sometimes revitalized. Admissions such as "I feel like a heavy weight has been dropped from my shoulders," and "I should have left a long time ago," are common.

One that sticks in my mind is "I feel like I just got up from the dentist's chair."

Hazard 98: Resisting the Discomfort of Necessary Change

Solutions Seeking Problems: The Cost of Avoiding Learning

Learning a new approach and adapting to a different organizational culture requires the ability to critically evaluate what worked in the past, suspend judgment on what may be necessary in a different environment, and remain open to new possibilities. Resisting the discomfort of change and retreating into the false safety of old solutions to new and unevaluated problems, is a form of avoidance that can lead to derailment.

A frustrated executive provided a label for this form of avoidance when she described her new boss who was recently recruited from another company as "a solution looking for a problem." She went on to explain that this new executive isolated himself from interacting with experienced employees and demonstrated no interest in understanding the culture of his new firm. "He barricades himself in his office with a couple of cronies he brought with him, and they're blindly implementing a strategy that won't work here," she continued.

This ineffective leader came into his new role with a preconceived diagnosis of the company's problems along with a predetermined solution. He took the easy route and avoided assessing the relevance of his past experience to the reality of his new organization. His arrogance and aversion to the necessary discomfort of critical evaluation and subsequent learning created blinders that negated the need to actually interact with customers and employees before taking action. In his case, the action he took involved implementing a centralized management structure, curtailing the autonomy of his division managers, and closing some profitable branch offices. The frustrated executive was right; the solution didn't fit the problem and the new leader's strategy was overruled by the board of directors. Soon after, he was asked to resign—a casualty of derailment by avoiding the opportunity to learn.

CEOs, too, can succumb to derailment by avoiding learning and relying on locked-in biases and inappropriate organizational paradigms. In his profiles of five CEOs, Irwin (2009) provides two examples. Bob Nardelli, CEO of Home Depot, derailed by attempting to transfer General Electric's management system into an inappropriate and unreceptive culture. Durk Jager was openly hostile to Procter & Gamble's existing culture and avoided understanding its power. He, too, derailed.

Hazard 99: Focus on Comfortable, Irrelevant Activities

Failure to Launch: The Surgical Derailment of a Physician

Some leaders who derail by avoidance don't engage with their employees and escape into tangential activities simply because they find themselves in the wrong job for the wrong reasons. They compensate for their role discomfort and poor choice by avoiding the hard work of actually leading. In the title words of a 2006 romantic comedy film they suffer a "failure to launch." The aborted launch is most often caused by poor selection criteria and their own unrealistic expectations. Many leaders are selected based on the fallacy that the best technical contributors will automatically evolve into the most competent leaders. Some technical professionals are seduced into accepting leadership roles by unrealistic expectations of money, status and power. What sometimes happens is that the organization loses a superb professional and gains a frustrated, derailment prone, ineffective leader who resists the hard, against-the-grain, work of moving away from their past conditioning. That was the case with Dr. Porter.

Dr. Porter was an excellent orthopedic surgeon who was promoted to the chief operating officer of a growing regional health care system. In an unusual performance appraisal (he rarely did them), his boss, the CEO and board chairman, used the words "distracted"—"withdrawn"—"dejected" and "irritable" to describe his new and changed behavior. He indicated that Dr. Porter didn't meet with his employees, couldn't make tough decisions, and had reverted to spending more time back in clinical practice than managing his organization.

In the subsequent months, it became clear both to Dr. Porter and his boss that it wasn't working; he was well down the path of derailment by avoidance. The precision, clinical protocols and clarity of the operating room did not translate into the ambiguity and interpersonal issues that accompanied his leadership role. As part of an ill-conceived development plan two years previously, Porter completed a quantitatively oriented evening MBA program at a local university and graduated with the mistaken impression that management, like orthopedic surgery, was much more of a science than an art.

The system needed competent surgeons more than it needed poor leaders and, with help, Dr. Porter eventually came to see his leadership derailment as a positive. He concluded that he took the job for the wrong reasons—the status and the money—and that he was much happier and more productive as a clinical practitioner.

Porter's experience illustrates two realities. First, in order to be effective as a leader, one has to be motivated by the work itself, not its status or financial trappings. Inappropriate motivation leads to distraction, avoidance, and eventual derailment. Secondly, people derail from leadership roles because they are unable to pay the price of admission and are unwilling to admit that they are in the wrong job.

Perspective and Advice

- If you are a happy, challenged, and productive individual contributor, think long and hard before accepting a management role that takes you out of your comfort zone. There may be more money and status involved, but are you really willing to pay the dual price of dropping your technical and professional orientation and moving into the ambiguous, conflict-ridden, pressure cooker world of organizational leadership? Don't be seduced by either praise or promises. Look before you leap. What you may see are the type of duties and responsibilities you like to avoid. You have the opportunity to avoid them now by saying no. If you accept the job, then try to avoid them, you will derail.
- If you are involved in leadership selection, beware the trap of selecting the best technical performer and making her a leader. You may gain a poor leader who avoids the tough challenges and lose a great individual contributor who took the job only because she was seduced by money and status.
- If you assume a leadership position in a new organization, take the time and expend the energy to really understand the culture and

the customer preferences before attempting radical changes or trying to force fit a system that worked with your previous employer. Regardless of your past successes, the price of avoiding the necessary investment in learning could be your job. You wouldn't go to a physician who didn't diagnose before prescribing so don't be leader without the same approach. A misdiagnosed medical issue could be hazardous to your health. Entering a new position with a preconceived solution to an undiagnosed problem will definitely be hazardous to your organization's health and put you on a route to derailment.

- If you are on a board or an executive search committee make sure that the ability to diagnose, learn, and understand your corporate culture is a key selection criterion. Don't repeat the mistake of many selection committees and pick someone solely based on their success in a different firm with a different culture. Selecting someone without assessing and valuing their ability to learn may result in reconvening your committee sooner than you'd like.
- If you are a leader who has lost his spark and lack the energy or enthusiasm to engage in a helping relationship with your employees, you may be a victim of terminal disengagement. The symptoms are sadness, isolation, self-absorption, and generalized anger. Unprocessed anger tends to turn inward and many see it evolving into depression. You could have difficulty seeing or accepting any of these symptoms. But, if there is any hint of them, seek help. Even though you may have the connections to hang on to your job, you're not doing yourself or your organization any good by sucking it up and attempting to survive. You may need more, but at minimum you need a fresh start in a different environment. Don't wait, find someone you trust and talk to them.
- If you work with a terminally disengaged leader, find a way to intervene and do it quickly. By avoiding his leadership responsibility he is harming his employees. By ignoring his mental health he is harming himself.

Appendix A:
The Derailment Risk
Assessment Inventory

The Derailment Risk Assessment Inventory is a self-assessment that asks you to evaluate your on-the-job behavior. Your answers will help measure your risks of career derailment and provide a frame of reference for behavioral changes that will minimize the chances of your career coming off the tracks. Please respond the way you actually behave, not the way you think you should behave. The more honest you are, the more you will benefit.

Directions

What follows are 70 statements concerning your organizational behavioral patterns. Some of the statements may seem similar but respond to each one. Read each item carefully, then using the scale of 1 to five, circle the number that best describes your on-the-job behavior.

Derailment Risk Assessment Inventory

Response Key:
1 = I *almost always* behave this way.
2 = I behave this way *most of the time*.
3 = I behave this way *some of the time*.
4 = I *occasionally* behave this way.
5 = I *almost never* behave this way.

1. I am aware of the political climate in my workplace and adjust my behavior accordingly.   1 2 3 4 5
2. When in meetings and conferences, I adhere to professional standards.   1 2 3 4 5
3. I make it clear that I will not engage in sexual relationships with my co-workers   1 2 3 4 5
4. I factor political realities into my ideas and strategic choices.   1 2 3 4 5
5. I display my best and most politically correct behavior in public meetings.   1 2 3 4 5
6. I abstain from sexual liaisons in my workplace.   1 2 3 4 5
7. I don't advocate ideas or practices that no longer fit the values and strategies of my organization.   1 2 3 4 5
8. I refrain from criticizing colleagues and organizational practices in meetings and conferences.   1 2 3 4 5
9. I immediately shut down any attempts by co-workers to engage in inappropriate sexual behavior.   1 2 3 4 5
10. I regularly confide in a trusted colleague to help me assess any self-sabotage in my organizational behavior.   1 2 3 4 5
11. I actively seek feedback from others.   1 2 3 4 5
12. I consciously monitor and seek feedback on the image I'm projecting.   1 2 3 4 5
13. I continually find ways to share my goals and objectives with others.   1 2 3 4 5
14. I seek to understand, evaluate, and learn from feedback.   1 2 3 4 5
15. I am aware of the image I need to project to grow and develop in my organization.   1 2 3 4 5
16. I am aware of the impact of my non-verbal communication and actively monitor it.   1 2 3 4 5
17. I don't argue with or belittle feedback I receive.   1 2 3 4 5
18. I adjust the image I project so that it reflects the values and preferences of my organization.   1 2 3 4 5
19. I am aware of my mental models and consciously share them.   1 2 3 4 5
20. I seek the perspectives of others to help me see myself the way others do.   1 2 3 4 5

21. I assess alternatives and evaluate options before making decisions or taking action.	1 2 3 4 5
22. I don't allow my feelings or emotions to block me from taking necessary action.	1 2 3 4 5
23. I don't get bogged down in unnecessary analysis before making decisions and taking action.	1 2 3 4 5
24. I seek the opinions and ideas of others before making decisions.	1 2 3 4 5
25. I'm able to make the hard decisions regardless of their impact on people.	1 2 3 4 5
26. I don't repress or ignore my feelings and emotions when considering actions that affect others.	1 2 3 4 5
27. I factor in strategic considerations and the impact on others before moving to action.	1 2 3 4 5
28. I can set aside my feelings and emotions in order to make necessary decisions.	1 2 3 4 5
29. I don't suffer from analysis paralysis and am able to make timely decisions.	1 2 3 4 5
30. I seek the advice of others when my experience and instincts don't seem to fit problems.	1 2 3 4 5
31. I own up to my mistakes.	1 2 3 4 5
32. I don't engage in abusive or intimidating behavior.	1 2 3 4 5
33. I refrain from excessive multitasking.	1 2 3 4 5
34. I am comfortable changing decisions based on new information.	1 2 3 4 5
35. I am considerate of the schedules and priorities of others.	1 2 3 4 5
36. I don't get bogged down on one set of activities to the exclusion of others.	1 2 3 4 5
37. I'm able to let go of previously held ideas when shown better options.	1 2 3 4 5
38. I don't use my power to force people to do things.	1 2 3 4 5
39. I avoid frenzied activities and over scheduling.	1 2 3 4 5
40. I access others to help me understand any disconnection between my behavioral preferences and the needs of the organization.	1 2 3 4 5
41. I don't hold grudges against other people or other functions.	1 2 3 4 5
42. I don't make decisions based on untested assumptions.	1 2 3 4 5
43. I understand the way national culture shapes values.	1 2 3 4 5
44. I find ways to vent my day-to-day frustrations before they impair my judgment.	1 2 3 4 5
45. I discard past practices that no longer make sense.	1 2 3 4 5
46. I tailor my management approach based on national cultural practices.	1 2 3 4 5

47. I don't wait to get even with other people or functions. 1 2 3 4 5
48. I don't make promises I can't keep. 1 2 3 4 5
49. I don't belittle cultural practices that are different from those of my home country. 1 2 3 4 5
50. I test the validity of the way I see other people and different functions by consulting with others. 1 2 3 4 5
51. I'm able to discard practices that worked in the past but no longer fit. 1 2 3 4 5
52. I create work groups that are diverse in the way they gather data and make decisions. 1 2 3 4 5
53. I help work groups support and help other units in the organization. 1 2 3 4 5
54. I don't only rely on the functional skills that got me to my present level to conceptualize problems and formulate solutions. 1 2 3 4 5
55. I create a team environment that encourages diverse opinions and open discussion. 1 2 3 4 5
56. I don't tolerate sarcastic and disparaging comments about other individuals or groups. 1 2 3 4 5
57. I'm not fixed on only one way of doing things. 1 2 3 4 5
58. I select people who are not mirror images of me. 1 2 3 4 5
59. I don't build my team by tearing down others. 1 2 3 4 5
60. I reach out to other organizational units to better understand their issues and perspectives. 1 2 3 4 5
61. I have tolerance for others who don't buy into my vision. 1 2 3 4 5
62. I work to keep my skills compatible with the evolving needs of the organization. 1 2 3 4 5
63. I actively engage with employees to help them deal with their day-to-day tasks. 1 2 3 4 5
64. I'm open to the possibility that my vision may not be correct. 1 2 3 4 5
65. I'm willing to invest time and energy to learn better ways of doing things. 1 2 3 4 5
66. I avoid spending time on non-essential activities that distract me from relevant issues. 1 2 3 4 5
67. I don't push my vision and strategy faster than the organization can absorb it. 1 2 3 4 5
68. I'm able to let go of familiar past practices that are not relevant to today's environment. 1 2 3 4 5
69. I don't drop out, I stay engaged. 1 2 3 4 5
70. I regularly reach out to others to gain their perspective on the fit of my behavior. 1 2 3 4 5

Scoring the Derailment Risk Assessment Inventory

Scoring Process:
1. Transfer the summed total for the items depicted across from the underlined derailment risk categories.
2. Add the category totals to arrive at the total for the derailment dimension.
3. Add the seven dimension totals to arrive at the overall total.

Self-Sabotage
Zipper Problems	Items 3, 6, 9	Total _____
Suicidal Meeting Behavior	Items 2, 5, 8	Total _____
Political Quicksand	Items 1, 4, 7	Total _____
Ability to Access Others	Item 10	Total _____
	Dimension Total	_____

Insight Deficit
Feedback Immunity	Items 11, 14, 17	Total _____
Image Mismanagement	Items 12, 15, 18	Total _____
Communication Constipation	Items 13, 16, 19	Total _____
Ability to Access Others	Item 20	Total _____
	Dimension Total	_____

Faulty Behavioral Wiring
Big Feet	Items 21, 24, 27	Total _____
Big Heart	Items 22, 25, 28	Total _____
Big Head	Items 23, 26, 29	Total _____
Ability to Access Others	Item 30	Total _____
	Dimension Total	_____

Incompatible Needs
Need to Be Right	Items 31, 34, 37	Total _____
Need to Be Nasty	Items 32, 35, 38	Total _____
Need to Be Busy	Items 33, 36, 39	Total _____
Ability to Access Others	Item 40	Total _____
	Dimension Total	_____

Warped Perceptions
Gunnysacking	Items 41, 44, 47	Total _____
Fantasy	Items 42, 45, 48	Total _____
Cross Cultural Blindness	Items 43, 46, 49	Total _____
Ability to Access Others	Item 50	Total _____
	Dimension Total	_____

Misdirected Loyalties
Functional Fixedness	Items 51, 54, 47	Total _____
Diversity Adversity	Items 52, 55, 58	Total _____
Sub-Unit Arrogance	Items 53, 56, 59	Total _____
Ability to Access Others	Item 60	Total _____
	Dimension Total	_____

Dysfunctional Traits
   Charisma   Items 61, 64, 67   Total _____
   Irrelevance   Items 62, 65, 68   Total _____
   Avoidance   Items 63, 66, 69   Total _____
   Ability to Access Others   Item 70   Total _____
                                                                Dimension Total _____
                                                                OVERALL TOTAL _____

Understanding Your Scores

There are no right or wrong answers. The Derailment Risk Assessment Inventory is a self-scoring, diagnostic instrument to help you evaluate the risk of coming off the track. No one is immune to all the hazards of career derailment and this structured assessment will help quantify the degree of risk and serve as a frame of reference for taking corrective action. What follows are general guidelines for interpreting your scores. These guidelines need to be tempered by your own context when answering the questions. In the final analysis, you are the best judge of the meaning of your answers.

The 7 Derailment Dimensions: Each derailment dimension is broken down into the three supporting categories and one "Ability to Access Others" item. To get a general perspective of your derailment prognosis, sum the four item totals and enter it in "Dimension Total." The scoring guidelines are: 10–14 (low risk); 15–20 (slight risk); 21–30 (moderate risk); 31–40 (high risk); 40 + (very high risk). For scores above 25 it is highly recommended that the chapters dealing with that dimension be referenced for perspective and advice.

The 21 Categories: To get a clearer reading on specific category risks, it is necessary to review the score for each one. Scores of five or less represent a low derailment prognosis. Scores of 6–9 a moderate risk, and scores above 9, a substantial risk. For any score above 8, it is recommended that the chapter dealing with that category be referenced for perspective and advice.

The Ability to Access Others Items: A primary strategy for staying on track and overcoming the hazards of career derailment involves accessing others, seeking their advice, feedback, and perspectives. Each derailment category contains an item measuring the ability and effort to seek out others. Scores of 3–5 are strongly indicative of the need to find more ways to reach out to for guidance and perspective.

The Overall Total: Summing the 7 dimension totals will result in the overall total. This gives a very general indication of your risk of career derailment. Scores above 175 are indicative of the need to take action to reduce your potential for derailment.

Appendix B: The 21 Derailment Risk Categories

Derailment Risks	What to Do About Them
1. **Zipper Problems:** Sexual relationships in the work place.	No matter how tempting, exciting, or flattering, there is a simple one word mandate: "Don't!"
2. **Suicidal Meeting Behavior:** Allowing brief unguarded moments of irresponsible behavior in public meetings to permanently damage your career.	Regardless of the seductive aura of informality don't be misled. People are watching and they will remember. Be on your best behavior.
3. **Political Quick Sand:** Misreading the political climate, over-advocating a previous approach, and lack of flexibility	Look before you leap. What worked in the past may not fit. Learn to read the signs and let go of strategies that don't fit the organizational & values.
4. **Feedback Immunity:** Inability to "hear," value, or learn from feedback.	Find and contract with a trusted "truth teller"
5. **Image Mismanagement**: Lack of awareness or concern over the image you project.	Assess the image you're projecting and against the image you desire. You will need help to make changes.
6. **Communication Constipation:** Not sharing dreams, goals, mental models or development needs. Lack of competence and awareness of non-verbal communication.	Take the time and expend the effort to make goals and mental models clear. Learn the power and develop the skills to harness non-verbal communication.
7. **Big Feet:** A bias for taking action, unregulated by thinking or feeling.	Slow down. Find ways to access others and listen to their thoughts and feelings. Unguided missiles crash. Don't be one.
8. *A Big Heart:* Allowing empathy and emotional support to block rational analysis and decision making.	Management is an against the grain experience for the big-hearted. To survive you need to cultivate a support system where you can externalize your feelings and emotions.
9. *A Big Head:* Over-reliance on analysis combined with a deficit in taking action & emotional intelligence.	Difficult though it may be, you need to develop interpersonal competence, empathy, and comfort with the ambiguity and unpredictably of human behavior. You will need the help of a skilled coach.

Derailment Risks	What to Do About Them
10. *The Need to Be Right:* Individual, non-collaborative decision making and stubborn adherence to decisions despite conflicting evidence or other opinions.	Have the courage to drop the veneer of invulnerability and personal "rightness" and open yourself up to others.
11. *The Need to Be Nasty:* Driven by an ingrained aggressive, intimidating and abrasive leadership style.	Muster up the courage to look in the mirror and don't back away from what you see. It will be difficult and you'll need help but unless you make some fundamental changes it will only be a matter of time before you're gone.
12. *The Need to Be Busy:* Distracting multi-asking mania at lower levels and counter productive "activity traps" toward the top.	Drop the Facade of Busyness. Organizations want people who can focus, appear calm, and have time to authentically connect with other people. Beware of becoming caught in an activity trap. Seek external help to escape.
13. *Gunnysacking:* Accumulating a heavy burden of unvented feelings, emotions, and frustrations.	Keep your gunnysack light by continually externalizing its contents. Don't allow it to get too heavy and overwhelm you.
14. *Fantasy:* Judgments and actions warped by false and unrealistic perceptions.	Cultivate healthy self-doubt and have the courage to engage in regular reality checks by accessing others.
15. *Cross Cultural Blindness:* Inability to visualize the different ways country and regional cultures shape employee values and motivation.	Learn the basic concepts of cross-cultural research and apply them to your leadership practice.
16. *Functional Fixedness:* Applying your functional skills & strategic orientation to a problem that requires a different perspective.	Have the courage to move out of your functional comfort zone & more objectively diagnose and respond to problems and strategic choices.
17. *Diversity Adversity:* Creating narrow, non-diverse work groups and teams.	Resist the temptation to build a team of people who think, look, and act like you. The most powerful and creative teams are differentiated by their diversity.
18. *Sub-Unit Arrogance:* Building a team around hostility, superiority and sarcasm directed at other organizational units or individuals.	Establish and reinforce a norm of accommodating and supporting other organizational units. Know that building a team based on a foundation of arrogance is fragile, self-serving, and it will ultimately crumble.
19. *Charisma:* Inability to modify the "rightness" of a vision or values. Delusion of nvincibility and low tolerance for dissension.	Seek and accept external evaluation of the validity of your vision & openness to feedback. Don't become a victim of the adulation of followers.

The 21 Derailment Risk Categories

Derailment Risks	What to Do About Them
20. *Irrelevance:* Skills, style, and values no longer fit the current organizational culture.	Engage in an honest self-assessment of the fit between your competencies and those valued by your organization & have the courage and discipline to make changes.
21. *Avoidance:* Unwillingness to authentically engage with employees and escape into non-essential diversions.	If you lack the energy or enthusiasm to engage in a helping relationship with your employees seek help. Even if you have the connections to hang on to your job, you're not doing yourself or your organization any good by attempting to survive.

Appendix C: The 99 Derailment Hazards

Listed in Order of Appearance in the Text
1. Sexual relationships between boss and subordinate.
2. Sexual entanglements between hierarchical levels.
3. Lateral sexual entanglements.
4. Status based illusion of immunity.
5. Unguarded public outbursts.
6. Open public conflict
7. Putting a bad entry in the unwritten career "book."
8. Underestimating the impact of "normal" meeting behavior.
9. Inability to let go of what worked in the past.
10. Belief in executive invulnerability.
11. Inability to read the structural tea leaves.
12. Self-inflicted political quicksand.
13. Unwillingness to "hear" feedback.
14. Feedback blocking defense mechanisms.
15. Lack of courage and wisdom to look in the mirror and absorb what's revealed.
16. Ignoring corrective feedback.
17. The trap of the "let me give you feedback" approach.
18. Lack of courage to resist defense mechanisms and seek out the underlying message.
19. Unawareness of an ineffective image.
20. Allowing the need to be liked to eclipse an ineffective image.
21. Viewing image management as selling out or inauthentic.
22. Falling victim to the impostor syndrome.
23. Not sharing plans and dreams.
24. Hiding development needs.
25. Lack of non-verbal attending behavior.
26. Inability to engage in open, caring, other-centered dialogue.
27. Taking action based on untested assumptions.
28. Blindly following the signals of a big-footed boss.
29. A ready-fire-aim style.
30. Fabricating a problem to justify taking action.
31. Shallow diagnosis—self-serving analysis.
32. Inability to make "hard" people decisions.

33. Avoiding necessary conflict.
34. Over-reliance on feelings and emotions.
35. Against-the-grain seduction by status and money.
36. Over-reliance on data: under- reliance on feelings.
37. Addiction to analysis.
38. Inability to drop an affinity for macho, analytical, controlling cultures.
39. Left-brain bias.
40. Perception of management as a science.
41. Fear of softness.
42. Narrow scope—compulsion to measure and control a single paradigmatic box and an inability to think outside it.
43. Linking self esteem to unilateral rightness.
44. Letting ego and arrogance block valid data and other opinions.
45. Rigid adherence to outdated policies and procedures.
46. Inability to tolerate the vulnerability of asking others for help.
47. An abusive, intimidating style.
48. Adopting a nasty boss as a role model.
49. Attempting to fix the root motivational drive of a chronic nasty.
50. Confusing busyness and multitasking with productivity.
51. Lack of interpersonal competence.
52. Phony busyness.
53. Activity traps.
54. Cost cutting mania.
55. An obsession for busyness.
56. Colluding to project an artificial image of productive work.
57. Bottling up unresolved emotions until they explode.
58. Allowing repressed emotions to permanently damage perceptions.
59. Unrealistic anticipation of magical change.
60. The Ponzi fantasy.
61. Making undeliverable promises.
62. Belief in a one-dimensional score card.
63. Cross-cultural managerial incompetence.
64. Not understanding the leadership implications of cross-cultural research.
65. Prematurely pressing for change.
66. Inappropriate social distance.
67. Insensitivity to power-distance values.
68. Imposing individualistic values on collectivist cultures.
69. Rigid adherence to a sequential time orientation.
70. Functional blinders.
71. Strategic blinders.
72. Style blinders.
73. Retreating to a past comfort zone.
74. Creating a team of puppets.
75. Intolerance of outliers.
76. Top-down, one-dimensional leadership.
77. Lack of focus and concern over how the group operates.
78. Leaders who don't solicit or value team feedback.

79. Joyless and stressful meetings.
80. Overlooking style and decision-making diversity when creating teams.
81. Building a team by demeaning other teams
82. Fostering animosity toward higher organizational units
83. Over-identification with a high-performing sub-system.
84. Loyalty and commitment to own work: indifference to the organization as a whole.
85. Naïve sub-unit loyalty.
86. Completely trusting a charismatic leader.
87. Membership in a business cult.
88. Premature transformational leadership.
89. Transformational overload.
90. Inability to adjust to the new employment contract.
91. Failure to develop and maintain marketable skills.
92. Having values and know-how of use to only one organization.
93. Inability to drop a command-and-control orientation.
94. A dependency relationship with one company or industry.
95. Succumbing to disengagement.
96. Working for a disengaged leader.
97. Self-absorption.
98. Resisting the discomfort of necessary change.
99. Focus on comfortable, irrelevant activities.

References

Adamson, R. 1952. Functional Fixedness as Related to Problem Solving: A Repetition of Three Experiments. *Journal of Experimental Psychology* 44: 288–291.

Argyris, C. 1970. *Intervention Theory and Method: A Behavioral Science View.* Reading, Mass.: Addison-Wesley.

Bass, B., and Avolo, B. Eds., 1994. *Improving Organizational Effectiveness Through Transformational Leadership.* Thousand Oaks, Calif.: Sage.

Belbin, M. 2010. *Team Roles at Work,* 2nd ed. New York: Routledge.

Benne, K., and Sheats, P. 1948. Functional Roles of Group Members. *Journal of Social Issues* 4: 41–49.

Bennis, W. 2003. *On Becoming a Leader,* 2nd ed. New York: Basic Books.

Best, S. 2002. *Introduction to Politics and Society.* London: Sage, 2002.

Blanchard, K., and Miller, M. 2013. *The Secret: What Great Leaders Know and Do.* San Francisco: Berrett-Koehler.

Briggs Myers, I. 1998. *Introduction to Type,* 6th ed. Palo Alto, Calif.: Consulting Psychologists Press.

Burke, R. 2006. Why Leaders Fail: Exploring the Dark Side. *International Journal of Manpower* 27 (1): 91–100.

Burns, J. 1978. *Leadership.* New York: Harper & Rowe.

Carlson, N. 2013. Morale Is Dramatically Better Than It Was Under Andrew Mason. *Business Insider,* August 9. http:www.businessinsider.com/new-groupon-ceo-moral-is-dramatically-better-than-it-was-under-andrew-mason-2013-8.

Carr, M., Curd, J., Dent, F., Davda, A., and Piper, N. 2011. *Ashridge MBTI Research into Distribution of Type,* 2nd ed. Berkhamsted Hertfordshire, UK: Ashridge Business School.

Chalre' Associates. 2014. Main Reasons for Expatriate Failure, March. http://chalre.com/hiring_managers/reasons_expat_failure.htm.

Clance, P., and Imes S. 1978. The Impostor Phenomenon in High Achieving Women: Dynamics and Therapeutic Intervention. *Psychotherapy: Theory, Research and Practice* 15 (3): 241–247.

CNN Moneytech. 2014. Ousted Yahoo Exec's Golden Parachute May Be a Record. January 17. http://money.cnn.com/2014/01/17/techno.

Covey, S. 1989. *The Seven Habits of Highly Effective People: Restoring the Character Ethic.* New York: Simon & Schuster.

Crabtree, S. 2013. Worldwide 13% of Employees Engaged at Work. *Gallup,* October 8. http://www.gallup.com/poll/165269/worldwide-employees-engaged-work.aspx.

Dotlich, D., and Cairo, P. 2003. *Why Ceo's Fail: The 11 Behaviors That Can Derail Your Climb to the Top and How to Manage Them.* San Francisco: Jossey-Bass.

Drucker, P. 2001. *The Essential Drucker: Sixty Years of Peter Drucker's Essential Writings.* New York: Harper-Collins.

Duke University. 2012. Textiles and Apparel, 2002. North Carolina in the Global Economy. http://www.ncglobaleconomy.com/textiles/overview.shtml.

Frommer, D. 2012. The Truth About Why Yahoo's CEO Got Fired. Read/Write.Com, May 16. http://readwrite.com/2012/05/16/the-truth-about-why-yahoos-ceo-got-fired.

Furnham, A. 2010. *The Elephant in the Boardroom: The Causes of Leadership Derailment.* Houndmills, U.K.: Palgrave Macmillan.

Glaser, J. 2014. Vital Instincts: The DNA of Healthy Conversations. *Leader to Leader* 74 (Fall): 49–54.

Goldenberg, S. 2008. Iraq War My Biggest Regret, Bush Admits. *Guardian*, December 2. http://theguardian.com/world/2008/dec/02/George-bush-iraq-interview.

Goldman, D. 2011. HP CEO Apotheker Fired, Replaced by Meg Whitman. *CNN Money/Tech*, September 2. http://money.cnn.com/2011/09/technology/hp_ceo_fired/.

Goldsmith, M. 2006. *What Got You Here Won't Get You There: How Successful People Become Even More Successful.* New York: Hyperion.

Goleman, D. 2006. *Emotional Intelligence: Why It Can Matter More Than IQ*, 10th ed. New York: Bantam.

Goodwin, D. 2005. *A Team of Rivals: The Political Genius of Abraham Lincoln.* New York: Simon & Schuster.

Grind, K. 2014. Bond King Loses Showdown at Firm. *Wall Street Journal*, September 27–28. http://www.wsj.com/articles/bond-king-bill-gross-loses-showdown-at-firm-1411773652.

Hall, E. 1966. *The Hidden Dimension.* New York: Anchor.

———. 1976. *Beyond Culture.* New York: Anchor.

Hammer, A. 2000. *FIRO B Technical Guide.* Palo Alto, Calif.: Consulting Psychologists Press.

Hastings, M. 2010. The Runaway General. *Rolling Stone*, July 8. http://www.rollingstone.com/politics/news/the-runaway-general-2010622.

Hayes, F. 2002. 35 Years of Tech Flops. *Computer World*, September 30. http://www.computerworld.com/article/2579257/35-years-of-tech-flops.html.

Hirsch, P. 1987. *Pack Your Own Parachute: How to Survive Mergers, Takeovers, and Other Corporate Disasters.* Reading, Mass.: Addison-Wesley.

Hoffman, E. 1994. *The Drive for Self: Alfred Adler and the Founding of Individual Psychology.* Reading, Mass.: Addison-Wesley.

Hofstede, G. 1980. Motivation, Leadership, and Organization: Do American Theories Apply Abroad? *Organizational Dynamics* 9 (1): 42–63.

Irwin, T. 2009. *Derailed.* Nashville Tenn.: Thomas Nelson.

Jensen, M. 2013. *HR Pioneers: A History of Human Resource Innovation at Control Data Corporation.* St. Cloud, Minn.: North Star Press.

Knowdell, R., Branstead, E., and Moravec, M. 1995. *From Downsizing to Recovery: Strategic Transition Options for Organizations and Individuals.* Palo Alto, Calif.: CPP Books.

Langley, M. 2003. *Tearing Down the Walls.* New York: Simon & Schuster.

Leider, R., and Shapiro, D. 2012, 3rd ed. *Repacking Your Bags: Lightening Your Load for the Good Life.* San Francisco: Berrett-Koehler.

Lenzer, R. 2008. Bernie Madoff's $50 Billion Ponzi Scheme. Forbes.com, December 12, 2008, http://www.forbes.com/2008/12/12/madoff-ponzi-hedge-pf-ii-in_rl_1212croesus_inl.html.

Levinson, H. 2006. *On the Psychology of Leadership.* Boston: Harvard Business School Publishing.

Libert, A. 1995. The Battle of Waterloo. *Military Subjects, the Hundred Days*, 1995–2004. http://www.napoleon-series.org/military/battles/hundred/c_chapterr.html.

Little, M. 2014. Bridgegate: What's the Scandal Ensnaring Chris Christie? *Los Angeles*

Times, January 9. http://articles.latimes.com/2014/jan/news/la-pn-bridgegate-christie-q-and-a-20140109.

McCall, M., and Lombardo, M. 1983. *Off the Track: Why and How Successful Executives Get Derailed, Technical Report 21*. Greensboro, N.C.: Center for Creative Leadership.

McClelland, D. 1987. *Human Motivation*. Cambridge, U.K.: Cambridge University Press.

McNamara, R. 1996. *In Retrospect: The Tragedy and Lessons of Vietnam*. New York: Vantage.

Mead, S. 1952. *How to Succeed in Business Without Really Trying: The Dastard's Guide to Fame and Fortune*. New York: Simon & Schuster.

NBC. *Meet the Press*. 2014. May 16. http://nbcnews.com/id/4499258/.

Noer, D. 1975. *Multinational People Management: A Guide for Organizations and Employees*. Washington D.C.: BNA Books.

_____. 1976. *Jobkeeping: A Hireling's Survival Manual*. Radnor, Penn: Chilton.

_____. 2008. A Comparison of Saudi Arabian and United States Learning Tactics. *International Journal of Management* 25 (1): 23–27.

_____. 2009. *Healing the Wounds: Overcoming the Trauma of Layoffs and Revitalizing Downsized Organizations*. San Francisco: Jossey-Bass.

_____, Pantania, J., and Leopold, C. 2006. The Impact of Culture on Coaching Behaviors: A Comparison of English, French, German, and Indian Managers. *Global Educational Journal*: 58–77.

_____, and Sternbergh, B. 2014. Top 10 Career-Limiting Leadership Behaviors. *Leader to Leader* 72 (Spring): 7–12.

_____, Valle, M., and Leopold, C. 2007. An Analysis of Saudi Arabian and U.S. Managerial Coaching Behaviors. *Journal of Managerial Issues* Summer XIX (2): 271–288.

Odiorne, G. 1974. *Management and the Activity Trap*. New York: Harper & Rowe.

Paczkowski, J. 2013. Groupon CEO "I Was Fired Today." *All Things D*, February 28. http://allthingsd.com/10130228/groupon-dumps-andrew-mason-as-ceo/.

Peter, L. 1969. *The Peter Principle: Why Things Always Go Wrong*. New York: William Morrow & Company.

Philbrick, N. 2010. *The Last Stand: Custer, Sitting Bull, and the Battle of the Little Big Horn*. New York: Penguin.

Pile, C., and Roberts, T. 2014. *Deus Ex Machina: The Progress of Secular Socialism*. New Orleans: Lanterns of Liberty.

Pulley, M. 1997. *Losing Your Job—Reclaiming Your Soul*. San Francisco: Jossey-Bass.

Roché, J. 2014. Conquering Impostor Syndrome: Lessons from Female Business Leaders. *Leader to Leader* 74 (Fall): 12–17.

Rubinstein, J., Meyer, D., and Evans, J. 2001. Executive Control of Cognitive Processes in Task Switching. *Journal of Experimental Psychology* 27 (4): 763–797.

Schnell, R., and Hammer, A. 1993. *Introduction to the FIRO in Organizations*. Palo Alto, Calif.: Consulting Psychologists Press.

Tang, R. 1987. Expatriate Assignments: Enhancing Success and Minimizing Failure. *Academy of Management Executive* 1 (2): 117–126.

Tichy, N., and Devanna, M. 1986. *The Transformational Leader*. New York: John Wiley & Sons.

Tomasko, R. 1987. *Downsizing: Reshaping the Corporation for the Future*. New York: AMACOM.

Trompenaars, F. 1993. *Riding the Waves of Culture: Understanding Cultural Diversity in Business*. London: The Economist Books.

Tuttle, B. 2013. The 5 Big Mistakes that Lead to Ron Johnson's Ouster at J.C. Penny. *Business Time*, April 9. http://business.time.com/2013/04/09/the-5-big-mistakes-that-led-to-ron-johnson's-ouster *At-Jc-Penny*.

Vaill, P. 1982. The Purposing of High Performing Systems. *Organizational Dynamics* (Autumn): 23–39.

———. 1989. *Management as a Performing Art.* San Francisco: Jossey-Bass.

Waldroop, J., and Butler, T. 2000. *The 12 Bad Habits That Hold Good People Back: Overcoming the Behavior Patterns That Keep You from Getting Ahead.* New York: Doubleday.

Weiner, T. 2015. *One Man Against the World: The Tragedy of Richard Nixon.* New York: Henry Holt.

Welch, J. 2013. Insights on Charismatic Leadership from the Heroes and Villains. *Leadership by the People*, June 19. http://www.leadershipbythepeople.org/Charismatic-Political-Leaders.php.

Woodward, B., and Bernstein, C. 1974. *All the President's Men.* New York: Simon & Schuster.

Zenger, J., and Folkman, J. 2009. Ten Fatal Flaws That Derail Leaders. *Harvard Business Review*, June 1. http://hbr.org/2009/06-ten-fatal-flaws.

Index

abrasive style: advice about 98–99; causes 95–96; danger as role model 94; hazards of attempting to fix 96; why users derail 94–95
accessing others 39, 47, 55, 67, 73, 80, 91, 98, 108, 116, 143, 185
action before reflection style: advice about 65–67; fabricating problems to justify action with 62; managerial example of 62–65; perils of working under 60; ready-fire-aim approach 61; self-serving analysis by 62; shallow diagnosis with 62–64; untested assumptions by 58
activity traps *see* need to be busy
Adamson, R. 136
addiction to analysis style: advice about 80–81; fear of softness with 79; left brain bias of 78; narrow scope 80; over reliance on data—under reliance on feelings in 75; practitioners of as endangered species 77–78; propensity to form controlling cultures with 78
Adler, A. 95
Agnew, S. 125
All the President's Men 112
Apotheker, L. 139
Apple 138–139
approach/avoidance career suicide 28–29
Argyris, C. 36
As You Like It 45

Baroni, B. 60
Bass, B. 166
Belbin, M. 145
Benne, K. 145
Bennis, W. 2
Bernstein, C. 112
Biden, J. 154
big-hearted style: advice about 73–74; avoidance of necessary conflict with 70; dynamics of a derailment by 68–70; inability to make hard people decisions with 68; over-reliance on feelings and emotions with 71; seduction of status and money hazard with 71–73
Bin Laden, O. 162
Blanchard, K. 32
Bridgegate 60
Broadwell, P. 13

Burke, R. 2, 36, 120
Burns, J. 166
Bush, G.W. 62
Butler, T. 68

Cairo, P. 70
Carter, J. 70
Center for Creative Leadership 1, 92, 146
charisma: advice about 169–170; characteristics of leaders with 162–163; danger of trusting leaders with 162; hazard of cult membership with 163–165; why leaders derail 165–166
Christie, C. 60
Churchill, W. 162
Clance, P. 45
Clinton, B. 13
communication constipation style: advice about 55–56; hazards 48; hiding developmental needs under 50–51; inability to engage in open dialogue by 53–54; lack of non-verbal attending behavior by 51–52
Control Data 156–157
conversational constipation 53–54
Cosby, B. 13
cost-cutting mania 103–104
Covey, S. 2, 144
Crey, S. 156–157, 160
cross-cultural hazards: advice about derailment by 133–134; expatriate failure rates 127; ignoring high and low cultural contexts 128–130; imposing individualistic systems on collectivist cultures 132–133; insensitivity to power-distance values 131–132; managerial incompetence example 125–127; misreading social distance 130; not understanding cross-cultural research 127–128; prematurely pressing for closure 129–130; rigid adherence to sequential time 133
Custer, G. 84, 87–88

De Castro, H. 23
derailment: macro-traits 36; the 99 hazards of 193–195; the 21 risk categories of 193–195
Derailment Risk Assessment Inventory 187–192
disengagement: advice about 184–185; characteristics of leaders 181–182; peril of working

for a disengaged leader 179; prevalence 179; terminal type 181, 185
diversity in work teams: advice about 150–160; danger of intolerance of outliers 146–147; hazard of top-down leadership 147; importance of style and decision making differences 148–149; lack of concern over group process 147
Don Quixote 175
Dotlich, D. 70
Drucker, P. 2, 162
dysfunctional trait categories 161

Edwards, J. 13
Ehrlichman, J. 150
Eikenberry, K. 154
Eisenhower, D. 92
emotional intelligence 34–35, 79
Engineering Research Associates 156
Evans, J. 101
executive bearing 41–43

Failure to Launch 183
fantasy hazards: advice about 123–124; one dimensional delusions of 122; Ponzi type 119–120; undeliverable promises in 120–122; unrealistic expectations in 117–119
faulty behavioral wiring categories 57
feedback: advice about 39–40; blocking defense mechanisms 33–34; courage to hear 39, 143; danger of lack of team usage 147; developmental and corrective applications 35–36; example of rejection 34–35; guidelines for giving 38–39; hazards of unwillingness to hear 32–33; ignoring corrective type dangers 36–37; pain and promise of 36; three hundred and sixty degree type 34, 47; trap of "let me give you" approach 37–38
FIRO-B 71, 145–146
Folkman, J. 33
Freud, S. 33
functional fixedness: advice about 142–143; definition 136; functional blinders 137–138; reverting to a past comfort zone under 140–143; strategic blinders 138–139; style blinders 139–140
Furnham, A. 95

Galvin, C. 70
Gandhi, M. 162
General Electric 183
Goldsmith, M. 21
good boss-bad boss trait comparison 97–98
Goodman, D. 150
Google 23
Gross, B. 27
Groupon 139–140
groups: difference from teams 144; maintenance and task roles 145
gunnysacking: advice about 115–116; case study 111–112; causing permanent damage by 112; definition 110; effects of bottled up emotions by 110–111; group venting 114–114; revenge by 113–114

Haldeman, H. 150
Hall, E. 128, 130
Hammer, J. 71
Hewlett-Packard 139
hierarchiology 171
Hitler, A. 162
hockey stick financial forecast *see* fantasy hazards
Hofstede, G. 125, 127–128
Holbrook, R. 154
Holding on and letting go 21–23, 89–90, 142
Home Depot 183
How to Succeed in Business Without Really Trying 102

IBM 127–128
image management: advice about 46–47; allowing need to be liked to block 43–44; example of positive change in 41–43; importance 41; imposter syndrome 45–46; method acting as strategy 46; view as selling out 44–45
Imes, S. 45
incompatible needs categories 83
insight deficit categories 31
irrelevance: advice about 177–178; focus on unimportant tasks 183–184; lack of marketable skills 173–177
Irwin, T. 182

Jager, D. 183
Janus Capital Group 28
JCPenney 138
Johnson, R. 138
Jones, J. 162

Kelly, J. 60
Kennedy, J. 162
King, M. 162
Koresh, D. 162

Lay, K. 166
layoffs: re-engineering cause 103; survivors 78, 180
learning: avoiding 88, 182; cost of resisting 183, 185
Lefkofsky, E. 140
Levinson, H. 95
Lincoln, A. 149–150
lint heads: definition 177; demise of in North Carolina 176–177; *see also* new employment contract
Little Big Horn 87–88
Lombardo, M. 35, 92, 120, 146

MacArthur, D 36–37
Madoff, B. 120, 166
management: big-footed style *see* action be-

fore thinking style; command and control hazard 175–176; differences from leadership 2; middle managers as endangered species 173–174; nasty style *see* abrasive style; perception as a science 79; as performing art 44–45
Manson, C. 162
Mason, A. 139–140
Mayer, M. 23
McCall, M. 35, 92, 120, 146
McChrystal, S. 154
McClelland, D. 71
McLuhan, M. 136
McNamara, R. 80
meeting behavior: advice about 19–20; causing entry in unwritten career book 19; dangers in normal meetings 18–19; derailment of top executive by 17–18; public outbursts in 16–17; results of joyless and stressful sessions 148
Meyer, D. 101
misdirected loyalty categories 135
Motorola 70
multitasking *see* need to be busy
Myers-Briggs Type Indicator 71, 148–149

Napoleon 87, 166
Nardelli, B. 183
need to be busy: advice about 107–108; danger of activity traps 102–103; fallacy of multitasking 102; masking necessity for interpersonal competence 101; as obsession 104–107; use to create artificial image 107
need to be right: advice about 91; blocking valid data 87–88; causing adherence to outdated policies 88–89; danger of linking self-esteem to 84–87
new employment contract 27, 81, 114, 171–173, 175, 177
new reality *see* new employment contract
Nixon, R. 112–113, 117, 149–150
Nobel Peace Prize 70
Norris, W. 156, 166

Obama, B. 13, 154
Odiorne, G. 100

Pacific Investment Management Company 27–28
Paulson, P. 42
The Peter Principle 171
Peters, L. 171
Petraeus, D. 13
political quicksand: advice about 29; hazards 21–29; inability to read structural tea leaves 24; top executive belief in invulnerability 23
Powell, C. 62
Procter and Gamble 183
psychological contract *see* new employment contract
Roché, J. 46
Rubinstein, J. 101

satisfaction surveys 180
Schnell, R. 145
self-absorbed leaders *see* disengagement
self-delusions 47
self-initiated derailment 25–29
self-sabotage categories 7
sequential time 133
sexual relationships in workplace: advice about 14–15; between boss and subordinate 8–9; between hierarchical levels 10; equal opportunity derailment factor 13; hazards 14–15; lateral liaisons 10–12; status-based illusion of immunity 12–13
Shakespeare, W. 45
Sheats, P. 145
Skilling, J. 166
Smothers Brothers Comedy Hour 42
Sokolich, M. 60
Spock 75
Star Trek 75
Sternbergh, B. 1
sub-unit arrogance: advice about 159–160; commitment to own work only 156–157; folly of building a team by demeaning others 152–153; hazard of fostering animosity toward higher level units 154; naïve loyalty 157–159; over-identification with high performing sub-system 154–156
synchronic time 133

A Team of Rivals 150
Thompson, S. 23
transactional leadership 166–167, 170
transformational leadership: definition 166; serial use 168–169; when premature application causes derailment 167–168
Trompenaars, F. 133
Truman, H. 36
truth teller 31, 98, 116

UNIVAC 156

Vaill, P. 45, 154–155, 160

Waldroop, J. 68
warped perception categories 109
Watergate 150
Waterloo 87
Weber, M. 162–163
Weiner, A. 13
Weiner, T. 112
Welch, J. 162
Whiz kids 80
Wild, O. 68
Wildstein, D. 60
Woods, T. 13
Woodward, B. 112

Yahoo 23–24

Zenger, J. 33

www.ingramcontent.com/pod-product-compliance
Ingram Content Group UK Ltd.
Pitfield, Milton Keynes, MK11 3LW, UK
UKHW042005140426
5217IPUK00015B/999